FREE WILL
THE BASICS

The question of whether humans are free to make their own decisions has long been contested and it continues to be a controversial topic today. *Free Will: The Basics* provides readers with a clear and accessible introduction to this central philosophical debate. It examines key questions such as:

- Does free will exist or is it an illusion?
- Is it possible to have free will if everything is determined?
- Can moral responsibility exist without free will?
- What can recent developments in science tell us about the existence of free will?

With detailed examples, a glossary of key terms, and suggestions for further study, *Free Will: The Basics* addresses the key debates without prejudice and is an essential read for anyone wishing to explore this challenging and philosophical problem.

Meghan Griffith is Associate Professor of Philosophy at Davidson College, USA. She specializes in free will and action theory.

The Basics

FREE WILL

THE BASICS

Meghan Griffith

LONDON AND NEW YORK

First published 2013
by Routledge
2 Park Square, Milton Park, Abingdon, Oxon OX14 4RN

Simultaneously published in the USA and Canada
by Routledge
711 Third Avenue, New York, NY 10017

Routledge is an imprint of the Taylor & Francis Group, an informa business

British Library Cataloguing in Publication Data
A catalogue record for this book is available from the British Library

Library of Congress Cataloging in Publication Data
Griffith, Meghan.
Free will : the basics / Meghan Griffith.
p. cm. – (The basics updated)
1. Free will and determinism. I. Title.
BJ1461.G75 2013
123'.5–dc23
2012025034

ISBN: 978-0-415-56219-5 (hbk)
ISBN: 978-0-415-56220-1 (pbk)
ISBN: 978-0-203-07690-3 (ebk)

Typeset in Bembo and Scala Sans
by Taylor & Francis Books

Printed and bound in Great Britain by the MPG Books Group

For my parents

CONTENTS

ACKNOWLEDGEMENTS

Many thanks to those who read and commented on draft material: Randolph Clarke, Kristopher Denio, John Fischer, Stephen Griffith, Robert Kane, Alfred Mele, Siobhán Poole, Saul Smilansky, Manuel Vargas, members of my Davidson College free will seminar (Spring 2012), and several anonymous reviewers for Routledge. Thanks also to Emma Hudson, Andy Humphries, Amanda Lucas, Siobhán Poole, and Rebecca Shillabeer for their help and guidance at various stages of the process. I would like to thank my wonderful family for their continuous love and support, especially my husband, Kris, and my parents, Erica and Stephen Griffith.

INTRODUCTION

As my mother always says, life is choices. Experience seems to back this up. From the time I woke up this morning, I made countless decisions: exactly when to get out of bed, whether to eat breakfast and what to eat, when to brush my teeth and so on. In my conscious life, I cannot seem to avoid making choices. Suppose I say, "I am tired of choosing all the time. I think I will just refuse to make a decision". Paradoxically, my refusal is itself a choice I make. I can't get out of choosing so easily. In fact, our lives are so marked by choices that some philosophers have claimed that this defines what and who we are. In other words, these philosophers say that we are beings who must constantly choose. And it could be that the choices we make determine, or at least largely shape, who we become. It is perhaps unlikely that whether I have toast or cereal for breakfast will contribute much towards shaping who I become. But of course, not all of my choices are of such a trivial nature. Sometimes I must make weighty decisions, such as whether to get married and to whom, what kind of career to embark upon, or whether to resist some sort of temptation in order to do what I think is morally right.

Because choices are such a pervasive and important part of our experience, it should come as no surprise that all sorts of thinkers and writers have chosen (!) to study the nature and significance of choice in human life. Even those who have not formally studied or written about these issues have most likely wondered or even worried about them at one time or another. But what, exactly, might someone be worried about? One very famous, much-discussed, and central concern is referred to as the problem of free will.

THE PROBLEM OF FREE WILL

What is the problem of free will? This question is probably somewhat misleading because there is not really just one problem relating to free will. There is a cluster of problems. But in general, the worry is over whether we *have* free will.

WHAT IS "FREE WILL"?

What do philosophers mean when they talk about "free will" and when they wonder whether we have it? This question is very difficult to answer, because the answer is itself a big part of the debate, as we shall see. For now, we might understand "free will" very roughly as the power to make choices, as discussed in the beginning of this chapter. Even this rough characterization might not be agreed upon by all philosophers who write about these issues, but we can use this characterization in order to see what some of the issues are. Just keep in mind that different proposed solutions to the problems of free will sometimes utilize different understandings of what free will really is.

WHY IS IT CALLED "FREE *WILL*"?

The term "free will" is sometimes used to distinguish the power of choosing from other kinds of freedom. For example, we often talk about political freedom, or freedom of speech. Even within discussions of the problem of free will, free will is sometimes distinguished from free *action*. The basic idea is that there might be a difference between my having an ability to choose and having an ability to carry out my choice. So, for example, perhaps I choose to have toast for breakfast, but on my way to the toaster, I am suddenly struck with paralysis so that I cannot do what I have chosen to do.

Philosophers throughout history have discussed different parts or faculties of the human mind (or soul). Sometimes the distinction is drawn between the "intellect" and the "will". The "intellect" is the part that reasons. The "will" is the part that chooses. So while my intellect reasons to the conclusion that eating toast would be good, it is my will that must take the final step in actually *choosing* to eat toast. Philosophers continue to debate to what extent the will does or should follow what the intellect says (though few current-day philosophers would actually put it in terms of "an intellect" and "a will"). Philosophers also disagree on the other issues involved – whether the mind has separate parts or faculties, or whether it is divided in this particular way, or even whether we have minds! Some philosophers might even disagree that choosing is the same as willing. But these debates, though interesting and important, can be put aside for now. The point here is just to illustrate what is generally meant by a "will". And for present purposes we can say that free will is some sort of ability or power to choose.

WHY IS THERE A "PROBLEM" AND WHAT IS THIS PROBLEM?

As mentioned above, the problem of free will usually centers on the possibility or probability of having free will. Can we have it? Is it likely that we do have it? We might think that it is just obvious that we do have free will. After all, as mentioned at the beginning of this chapter, we are constantly making choices. But the worry involves the nature of these choices. We are strongly inclined to think that what we choose is "up to us". But what if this is just an illusion? Think of a visual illusion, like a mirage. What if our experience of choosing, like a mirage, is not really what it seems to us to be?

What if, for example, I *had to* choose toast for breakfast even though it seemed to me at the time as if I could have chosen cereal? We might think it odd that I would somehow be necessitated to choose toast. What could necessitate such a choice (and presumably without my even knowing it!)? One of the main suggestions is that my choice could have been necessitated by a chain of causes.

Let us take as our starting point the fact that my choice is an event. There is a time at which I make a choice, and this is my choice-making event. What caused this event? We tend to think that my choosing toast just at that moment has some sort of explanation and that there was something that made it happen just when it did. Often (though maybe not always) when we search for explanations, we are searching for causes. A natural way of explaining the choice is in terms of my internal states. For example, certain desires and beliefs I had at the time may have caused me to make my choice just then. I wanted to eat, I believed that by choosing toast I could fulfill this desire, I remembered that I had cereal yesterday, so I wanted something different today, and so on. So perhaps my choice is necessitated by my desires and beliefs (or by some internal event relating to these desires and beliefs).

This may not seem all that problematic – and some philosophers will argue that it is not. After all, these are *my* desires and beliefs. Why should I be worried about choosing on the basis of them? Furthermore, I am probably aware of many of these desires and beliefs, so I do not seem to be operating under any illusions. But the problem arises when we keep tracing things backwards in time. Are my desires and beliefs up to me? If they are not, it seems that ultimately my choice is not up to me either, since it is necessitated by them. To oversimplify – if my wanting toast *makes me* choose it, and it is not up to me whether I want toast, then it seems as if my choice is not really a choice after all. It's just an illusion.

But why wouldn't it be up to me whether I wanted toast? Well, in terms of experience, I think we can all relate to having desires that we feel we cannot help having. But since the worry here is that our experiences might not be accurate guides to reality, let us look to other considerations. These considerations are similar to those already discussed. It seems that my coming to have certain desires and beliefs was caused and therefore necessitated by something. I do not have the desires and beliefs I have just out of the blue – do I? We tend to think there is a complex story involving my genetic make-up and all the things that have happened to me throughout my life so far. Perhaps I am predisposed to like toast because my parents like toast. And throughout my life, I have had enough opportunities to eat toast to realize that I like it. Maybe these and other factors combine to ensure that I will want toast just when I do (and that I will therefore choose it). On the picture we are discussing, we can look at these factors as playing out in terms of events of cause and effect. But for the most part, these factors are not up to me. Even if some of them are, they may have causes that are not. And those causes have causes. So eventually, we could theoretically trace a causal chain to a time before I was born, a time when surely nothing was up to me. If each event necessitates the next one in the chain, then my choosing toast was actually something that had to happen right when it did. The illusion is that I think it is up to me whether to choose toast, but really this was established before I was even born!

This is one facet of the problem of free will. The worry is that although I feel as if my choices are up to me, they are really already laid out by things that happened before – things that are not up to me at all. Roughly speaking, the idea that from any point in time the whole future is fixed – that is, that events can only unfold in exactly one way – is called **determinism**. Determinism is often characterized in terms of causes, but not always. For now, it is enough to say that in general, philosophers often worry that determinism would rule out the possibility of genuine free will.

But maybe we were wrong to suppose that my choices are caused like this. Perhaps they are spontaneous and do not come about as the result of prior events. So, for instance, the choice of toast isn't caused by anything at all. Or, perhaps my choices are caused by prior events, but these prior causal events do not necessitate what they cause. Maybe causes just influence the likelihood of their effects. For example, maybe my desire for toast causes my choice in the sense of influencing it without necessitating it. Maybe it just makes it more likely that toast will be chosen. Both of these solutions have been proposed by notable philosophers and we will talk about them in some detail later on.

Right now, we must consider another facet of the problem of free will that comes up as a result of considering the suggestions just mentioned. The worry on this side of the problem is that our choices become random or arbitrary in a troublesome way. Take first the suggestion that my choice is not caused at all. If that is true, it seems that the choice just pops into my head from nowhere. How is such an event something that is "up to me"? If my choice is not caused, we are inclined to think that nothing can explain why I chose the way I did. Philosophers worry about whether such seeming randomness deserves to be called "free will". After all, free will is supposed to denote some sort of power of choice. According to many (though certainly not all) philosophers, uncaused choices cannot really be choices. The idea is that they are not within our control since they supposedly come out of nowhere. In some senses, such "choices" seem to have nothing to do with us, since they don't flow *causally* from our thoughts and desires.

It is perhaps a more complicated matter to discuss the arguments against the second suggestion (that our choices are caused but not necessitated). We can save this for a later chapter. Suffice it to say that the worries about this second proposal are similar, but not identical, to those just discussed concerning the first. Some philosophers argue that there is still a troubling lack of control, even in spite of the claim that such choices are causally influenced by our beliefs and desires (since they are not wholly uncaused).

The above discussion is meant to show why the idea of free will is problematic. It is threatened by determinism, but it is also threatened from the other side (if we take determinism away). Although I have mentioned some proposed solutions very briefly, there is much more to be said about these solutions. There are also plenty of other proposals to consider. The above is just meant to illustrate the nature of the problem. Different kinds of solutions have been proposed throughout the history of philosophy. Solutions are still being proposed today. It might come as a surprise that many of the solutions say that we can have free will even if all our choices are necessitated! This kind of view is generally called **compatibilism**. It may be interesting to note that some (but not all) compatibilists even say that having our choices necessitated is the *only* way we can have free will.

At this point, if you are confused or wondering how the problem of free will could possibly be solved, you are in good company. Sometimes the problem of free will is said to be the most difficult of the major philosophical problems. Lots of solutions have been proposed, but as we will see, none of the proposals avoids serious objections.

WHY DOES IT MATTER?

The difficulty of the problem of free will is good for professional philosophers – it will keep many of them employed for some time to come. But does it matter outside the small world of philosophical research? Maybe it is just an interesting intellectual puzzle with no real importance in our lives. I do not think so. There are important reasons why someone might care, even beyond the world of academic philosophy.

MORAL RESPONSIBILITY

Though the two do not always overlap, free will is closely linked to **moral responsibility**. Many philosophers think that if there were no free will, there could be no moral responsibility. And many believe that if something was not done out of free will, the person who did it cannot be held morally responsible for it (there are some qualifications to this which will be discussed later). To say that someone is morally responsible is generally to say that he is praiseworthy or blameworthy for something he has done.

It is fairly natural for us to link free will and moral responsibility. And the prevalence and importance of doing so goes well beyond the walls of the university. The easiest way to see this is to consider certain kinds of legal cases. Legal responsibility is not exactly the same as moral responsibility, but since legal responsibility is often based on intuitions about moral responsibility, these examples can be used to get at the intuitiveness of linking free will and moral responsibility.

When someone is put on trial for a crime, the defendant is represented by an attorney or team of attorneys. These defense lawyers attempt various strategies on behalf of their client. Sometimes they attempt to cast reasonable doubt on the defendant's guilt. But it has become increasingly common for the defense to offer reasons that the defendant should not be held responsible, even though there is no doubt that the defendant performed the act in question. In other words, the defense says that its client is not to blame, even though she clearly committed the crime. For example, the defense might claim that their client should not be punished because some brain abnormality or medical condition necessitated her behavior and took away her free will. The idea is that we think it unfair to blame (and punish) someone if her choice or action was not up to her. We might remove her from society to protect others, but to the extent that we believe that she could not help what she did, we also tend to think that she should not be blamed. Obviously, philosophers do not agree on what constitutes free will, nor do they always agree on the relationship between free will and responsibility. This means that they may have different things to say about certain cases and about their connection to the problem of free will. But thinking about these kinds of cases can at least show us why many people associate free will with responsibility.

Though some philosophers will counsel against it, what if we generalize from this kind of legal case? If such a defendant is not blameworthy for the sole reason that what she did was not up to her, then wouldn't this be true whenever something is not up to the person? What if no one ever has free will and so nothing is ever up to anyone? Does that mean that no one is ever blameworthy? Wouldn't that also mean that no one is ever praiseworthy? And wouldn't that mean that you can never blame anyone who has wronged you, nor can you ever pat yourself on the back for doing something good?

The point here is that the problem of free will is not just an intellectual exercise. It is not just about choosing wheat toast over corn flakes. It potentially involves deep human concerns over praise and blame.

RELIGION

Sometimes the problem of free will arises as a result of the claim that God knows ahead of time everything we will do (called **divine foreknowledge**). There are also difficult issues in some religious traditions concerning predestination. But what I want to focus on now is the importance of the existence of free will to a central theological problem. This is the problem of evil.

Within the monotheistic tradition, there is a conception of God as perfectly good, all-powerful, and all-knowing. Many philosophers and others have worried about why there is suffering in the world if such a God exists. If God exists and is good, knows everything, and is powerful enough to do anything, why is there suffering? God would want to eliminate it, would know about it, and would be powerful enough to eliminate it. Sometimes this leads philosophers to claim that God does not therefore exist, or that God does not have all three of those characteristics. But there have also been many solutions offered by theologians and philosophers. These solutions attempt to preserve God's existence and God's status as perfectly good, all-knowing, and all-powerful. One of the most important solutions is based on the idea of free will. The general idea is that because God wants human beings to make free choices, suffering cannot be eliminated. Human beings with free will do bad things and cause the suffering of other beings. God could stop the suffering by taking away free will, but free will is thought to be more valuable.

But what if it turns out that the problem of free will cannot be solved? What if free will is just impossible? Perhaps free will is conceptually incoherent – that is, we cannot make sense of the kind of ability it is supposed to be. If free will is not possible, then one important solution to the problem of evil has been ruled out (though there are other solutions that could be given). Although the problem of evil is a big point of discussion for philosophers, it also matters to believers everywhere. Some people have even abandoned belief in God when faced with real suffering in the world.

Furthermore, suppose we believe that God rewards good behavior and punishes sin. If God is good, then it seems that God would only reward and punish according to what someone deserves. But if there is no free will, perhaps there is no moral responsibility. This means that God would be punishing people who could not help but do what they did and are therefore not responsible. As with the problem of evil, God's goodness is called into question.

Although not everyone (some important philosophers included) thinks that all matters of faith should be subject to rational argument, many believers might find it important to be able to give rational support for a belief in free will.

AUTHORSHIP

One prominent current-day free will theorist, Robert Kane, talks about how, in making choices, it is like we are writing the narrative of our lives. The general idea is that I am the author of my own story and I develop my character as I go.

Many of us place a high value on this sort of authorship. There is something very appealing about controlling one's own destiny in some important sense. It allows us to feel that our accomplishments are truly *ours*. All the efforts we put forth amount to something. We are not just being carried along by life's current, but are active participants in the way things unfold.

Someone does not need to be a philosopher to worry about whether her big job promotion is something she can give herself credit for, or whether it is really the result of factors outside her control. Someone does not need to be a philosopher to wonder whether he should regret being too timid in high school or whether this is just something that could not have been helped.

DO WE REALLY WANT OR NEED FREE WILL?

But with all that being said, it is also worth noting at this point that some people might believe that free will is overrated. For example, some people might take comfort in the idea that we do not have free will. It is sometimes appealing to believe that there is a way things had to happen, or even that there is a way things were supposed to happen. It can be quite reassuring to think that some big "mistake" was not really my fault, because the choice was not really up to me after all. Others might take comfort in believing that God's plan entails that we have no free will.

Furthermore, some might believe that we can have meaningful lives without free will. One notable current-day philosopher, Derk Pereboom, argues that we do not have free will. But he argues that we do not need it in order to have the kinds of things that matter to us. This view will be discussed later.

These kinds of considerations do not mean that the problem of free will does not or should not matter to these people. Those who are comforted by the prospect of a lack of free will might care about the problem because they want it to be shown that free will is impossible or unlikely. And those who think we do not need it will most likely want to know why so many assume that we do and why philosophers often argue over what kind of free will we want to have.

OVERVIEW OF THIS BOOK

In the chapters that follow, we will look at various attempted solutions to the problem and some of the major objections to these solutions. It is worth keeping in mind the reasons that someone might care about the success of these solutions. Along the way, we will also discuss some of the underlying issues, such as moral responsibility, alternative possibilities, and determinism. We will look at some recent claims from the sciences that are said to bear on the problem of free will. And finally, I will make some concluding remarks about where all of this leaves us.

Chapter 2 is all about **compatibility** and **incompatibility**. Can free will exist alongside determinism? Are the two compatible? In this chapter, we will discuss what it means to be a compatibilist or an incompatibilist. We will also discuss determinism. What is it? What does it mean to say that determinism is true? The chapter includes discussion of some of the reasons one might prefer compatibilism to **incompatibilism** or vice versa.

The following chapter, Chapter 3, is about moral responsibility and the important issue of alternatives. What is moral responsibility? What does it mean to be the kind of being that can be morally responsible? How does this relate to free will? This chapter also discusses the difficult but central issue of alternative possibilities. If I am morally responsible for something, it seems, at least on the surface, that what I did should have been avoidable. In other words, how can I be blamed if I had no alternatives? Some philosophers suggest that alternatives are required, but others dispute this. Chapter 3 discusses this debate.

Chapters 4, 5, and 6 lay out some of the most important current free will theories. Chapter 4 covers compatibilist theories – theories that hold that even if determinism is true, we can still have free will. Chapter 5 discusses incompatibilist theories – theories that hold that if determinism is true, we cannot have free will. The theories discussed in Chapter 5 include theories that support belief in free will and those that think we do not have free will. Chapter 6 involves a discussion of a few alternative theories. These are interesting current-day theories that do not fit neatly into the other categories.

These three chapters (4, 5, and 6) are organized by theory. For each theory, the view is first explained, then there is discussion of how this view is supposed to solve the problem of free will. This is followed by a discussion of objections to the view (criticisms made by other philosophers for why the view might not work). Some responses to these objections are also discussed.

Chapter 7 is about free will and science. There are a number of scientific experiments and theories that seem to have bearing on the issue of free will. This includes everything from causal determinism, to quantum physics, to animal behavior, to experiments in neuro-science. This chapter discusses some of these issues and talks about how we might approach them philosophically. Do these experiments really have the implications that are sometimes claimed for them?

Finally, Chapter 8 offers some concluding thoughts about where all of this philosophical discussion over free will gets us.

Each chapter is followed by a Further Reading section that gives suggestions for what to read if interested in pursuing a particular topic. Readings vary in difficulty and intended audience, but all are of high quality and should be useful to those who wish to pursue further study.

The end of this book includes a glossary of some of the more difficult and less familiar terms. Although many of these terms are defined within the chapters, they have been listed alphabetically in the glossary so that readers can easily turn to them as needed. Terms that can be found in the glossary are indicated in bold within the body of the text the first time they appear in a chapter.

FURTHER READING

For a good, article-length overview of free will with an extensive bibliography, see: Timothy O'Connor, "Free Will", in Edward N. Zalta (ed.), *The Stanford Encyclopedia of Philosophy* (Summer 2011 Edition), www.plato.stanford.edu/archives/sum2011/entries/freewill/.

For a current debate between four prominent free will theorists, see John Martin Fischer, Robert Kane, Derk Pereboom, and Manuel Vargas, *Four Views on Free Will* (Walden, MA: Blackwell Publishing, 2007).

For some excellent collections of articles on free will, see Robert Kane (ed.), *Oxford Handbook of Free Will*, 2nd edition (New York: Oxford University Press, 2011); Derk Pereboom (ed.), *Free Will* (Indianapolis, IN: Hackett Publishing, 2009); and Gary Watson (ed.), *Free Will*, 2nd edition (Oxford: Oxford University Press, 2003).

2

THE COMPATIBILITY ISSUE

In the previous chapter, I mentioned that the problem of free will generally concerns whether we have free will. But a lot of philosophers who write about free will discuss whether the concept of free will is *compatible* with the concept of **determinism**. Does determinism rule out free will? This might seem to be a question about whether we have free will, but actually, it is its own important question and someone can answer it without answering whether we have free will. It's not that the question of **compatibility** is unrelated to the question of whether we have free will, but the two questions are distinct. In order to understand this, we first must discuss what philosophers mean by compatibility.

COMPATIBILITY

Peanut butter and jelly. R2-D2 and C-3PO. Fred Astaire and Ginger Rogers. What do these pairs have in common? We might be inclined to say that each pair exemplifies compatibility. Peanut butter is compatible with jelly. Fred is compatible with Ginger. They "go together". Is this what philosophers mean when they ask whether two things (such as free will and determinism) are compatible?

On the one hand, when philosophers discuss whether two things are compatible, they are talking about whether these two things go together. But the notion is a bit more specific than this. Saying that two things "go together" can mean a number of things. It can mean that they complement one another nicely. It can mean that they are part of a set. Or, it can mean that they are *possible* together. It is this last sense that philosophers use. Here's an example that should highlight the difference. Take marshmallow fluff and tuna. We would ordinarily not call them compatible in the "complementing each other nicely" sense. But they are *possible* together. You *can* put marshmallow fluff on your tuna sandwich, though I hardly recommend it.

Notice that saying whether two things are possible together is not necessarily indicating whether either of the two things exists. For example, suppose a group of scientists is speculating that if we were to discover a planet with a certain type of atmosphere (perhaps relevantly similar to ours) then that planet's environment would be compatible with life. They could argue that a certain set of conditions would make life possible. Life and these conditions are compatible because they can "go together" in the sense that they are possible together. Other conditions – extremely high temperatures, for example – are believed to be incompatible with life because those conditions and life cannot exist together.

What's important to notice about this example, though, is that this conclusion itself does not tell us anything about whether such a planet exists. And if the planet does exist, we still do not know, just on the basis of our compatibility conclusion, whether the planet actually has (or had) life. It only tells us that if we found a planet like this, then life would be a *possibility* there. After figuring out the compatibility question, there'd be more work to do to actually prove the existence of such a planet and then see whether it *actually* has or had life.

Notice, though, that figuring out the compatibility issue is useful because it tells us what the possibilities are. Return to the opposite kind of case. Assume there are environmental conditions, such as extremely high temperatures, that are *incompatible* with life. Well, what this means is that if scientists discover a new planet with these conditions, then they already know life is impossible there. The existence of life has presumably already been ruled out. This is not to say that the scientists are infallible. They could end up being wrong about whether these conditions are incompatible with life.

The point is, if the conditions really are incompatible with life, then we know that life has been ruled out on such a planet. It's also possible that scientists might disagree with one another about which conditions are compatible or incompatible with life. That means that they might end up disagreeing about what the possibilities are upon the discovery of a new planet. But nonetheless, thinking about compatibility tells us something about what we think the possibilities are.

The compatibility issue with regard to free will and determinism is a bit like the example with the planet (though with a lot more disagreement about compatibility). But we might want to be a bit more precise still: instead of asking whether two things can "go together", let's ask whether two statements can both be true. If they can both be true together, then the statements are compatible. If they can't both be true together, then they are incompatible. Take, for example, the following two statements about me:

1 I am an only child.
2 I have a younger sister who really annoys me.

You should notice right away that (1) and (2) are incompatible statements. At least one of them must be false. But which one? Maybe both of them are false. In any case, you need more information in order to know which one is false or if both of them are false (in fact, both statements are false). But notice that you can tell whether the statements are incompatible before you find out whether either one is true.

Let's look at another example. This one is about Mr Jones:

3 Mr Jones works at Jonesville Middle School.
4 Mr Jones is not a teacher.

Although you might assume that someone who works at a school is a teacher, we of course all know that it's perfectly possible for some-one to work at a school and not be a teacher. Most schools have a number of employees who perform various important functions other than teaching. So we can see that statements (3) and (4) are compatible. They are compatible because they could both be true together. But knowing they are compatible does not tell you which, if either, is true. You need more information in order to know whether Mr Jones in fact works at the middle school and to know whether he is a teacher. Again, notice that you can figure out whether the two statements are compatible before you know whether they are true. Even if they were both false, they'd still be compatible. Compatibility is about the relationship between the two statements.

Let's apply this to free will. So we might characterize the existence of free will with the following statement:

(a) Human agents (i.e. persons) sometimes have free will.

(We'll say "sometimes" here since believing that human agents have free will does not have to mean that everyone has it all of the time. It would be implausible to think that everyone always acts freely. Very few, if any, philosophers believe that.)

Then, let's use the following statement to characterize the existence of determinism:

(b) Our universe operates according to determinism.

(More will be said shortly about how to understand "determinism".)

So the compatibility question is whether statement (a) is compatible with statement (b). Could a deterministic universe also be a place where human agents sometimes act with free will?

Like the example with the planet, notice that deciding on the compatibility issue tells us about the possibilities. For example, suppose after reading much philosophy I decide that free will is incompatible with determinism. At this point, I might have no idea about whether statement (a) is true or whether statement (b) is true. But I have decided that they can't both be true. So this tells me what I believe the possibilities are:

(i)   that we have free will, but the world is not deterministic, or
(ii) that the world is deterministic and we don't have free will, or
(iii) that we don't have free will and the world is not deterministic.

If I think free will and determinism are incompatible, I have ruled out that we have free will and the world is deterministic.

Of course, the **incompatibility** of statements (1) and (2) (about being an only child and having a younger sister) is uncontroversial and easy to spot. With free will and determinism, there is an enormous amount of literature and no consensus among philosophers as to whether determinism rules out (i.e. is incompatible with) free will.

In the rest of this chapter, we'll talk about what is usually meant by determinism, and then why someone might favor either **incompatibilism** or **compatibilism**.

DETERMINISM

WHAT IS DETERMINISM?

There are different kinds of determinism (these will be mentioned a bit later). But for the most part in this book, we'll be talking about the kind involving the **laws of nature**. In a very general sense, determinism of this sort is a thesis about the way the universe operates.

Though there are some philosophers who disagree, philosophers and scientists generally believe that our universe operates under certain natural laws – these include laws of gravity, motion, energy, and so on. Laws are often understood as "**exceptionless regularities**". In other words, a law basically tells us that things always happen a certain way (in certain conditions) without exception. Sometimes laws of nature are understood as *making* things in the world happen. So, for example, someone who holds this view might say that the law of gravity makes things fall. But other philosophers think that laws themselves do not *do* anything, they just tell us the way things always happen. So, on this latter view, the law of gravity just tells us how bodies will always act under certain conditions. There are many theories about the laws of nature and we won't be able to get into the difficult and thorny issues here. For our purposes, we can just say that this kind of determinism generally involves a belief in exceptionless laws of nature of one kind or another. Those who think determinism is false, on the other hand, need not deny that there are laws of nature. It's just that these laws do not necessitate everything that happens.

So what is determinism then? Here is a standard characterization:

Determinism: the past and the laws of nature necessitate a unique future.

What this basically means is that given everything that has happened, and given the laws of nature, the future is fixed to be the way it is going to be – that is, it can only happen in one way. So, if determinism is true, *everything* that will happen next week is already determined, as is everything that will happen next month, next year, and so on. So it's not just that certain events are fated to happen no matter what leads up to them. Instead, the entire sequence must happen exactly as it does. It's also crucial to point out that human beings and their actions would not be immune to the effects of determinism. I am assuming that human agents operate within the natural world and are thus subject to it. If there are exceptionless laws of nature, it stands to reason that our bodies – including our brains – would have to obey them. So this means that if determinism is true, then it's determined already whether I'll go to the gym tomorrow and exactly how many times (and when) I'll blink next Wednesday.

So if determinism is true, everything is determined. But determined by whom? Not really by anyone (except maybe God, if one believes in God as the source of the laws of nature). The idea is that if there are deterministic laws of nature, then given certain circumstances, certain kinds of events will always follow certain other kinds of events. One of the easiest ways to think about this is in terms of cause and effect. In fact, sometimes this kind of determinism is called "causal determinism".

For example, if causal determinism is true, then every time a ball in certain circumstances is hit by another with a certain force, it will roll away with a certain trajectory. The second ball must roll just as it does. Likewise, the first ball had to roll just as it did, due to whatever caused *it* to roll (perhaps a pool cue or a third ball). Something caused that pool cue to move and something caused its cause and so on. All the causal factors necessitate exactly what will happen at each stage. Thus, these causal chains go back all the way to the beginning and continue on into the (determined) future.

DETERMINISM VERSUS THE PRINCIPLE OF UNIVERSAL CAUSATION

This brings us to a discussion of the relationship of the theory of determinism to the notion of cause and effect. It is a tricky matter to spell out the exact relationship between cause and effect and determinism.

One reason this is so difficult is that philosophers have been debating for centuries just how to understand what a cause is. As mentioned above, many philosophers will understand determinism in terms of cause and effect – as causal determinism. Others will omit the word "causal" and talk about determinism in terms of laws of nature (nomological determinism – "nomological" refers to the natural laws – or just determinism). We need not worry too much about these issues here.

But we do need to worry about a certain thesis that has often been confused with determinism. This is the thesis that "every event has a cause". For a long time, many philosophers thought that if every event has a preceding cause, then this is basically saying that every event is determined or necessitated by this cause. And this cause is determined or necessitated by a preceding cause and so on. So the thought was that this "**Principle of Universal Causation**" – as it is sometimes called – was the same as determinism.

At first glance, this seems to make sense. After all, if every event that occurs is caused by another event, then it seems that there are just unbroken causal chains of determined events with no "wiggle room" for anything to go differently. If it's false that every event has a cause, on the other hand, then maybe we'd have this "wiggle room". If there could be some uncaused events, then these events would not be predetermined by those events that came before. Being uncaused, no prior events or causes would "force" them to happen. Looking at the time before such an event, we would be able to say that it might happen or it might not. There would be nothing in the pipeline that would force the issue one way or the other. You will notice that if there are any events like this, then determinism, as a theory about the universe, appears to fall apart. There is not a fixed future because these uncaused events are not the inevitable result of what comes before them. The falsity of universal causation seems to imply the falsity of determinism.

But as plausible as it seems to equate universal causation and determinism, they aren't actually equivalent, since it is possible to think determinism is false, but universal causation is true. The falsity of determinism does not necessarily imply the falsity of universal causation. Someone might believe that every event has a cause, but think that the future is not thereby fixed by the past and the laws of nature. This may sound counterintuitive at first, but there are a couple of interesting reasons that someone might believe this. For example, someone might believe that at least some causes do not necessitate their effects. Sometimes this is discussed in terms of **probabilistic causation** – causes making their effects more likely, rather than making them 100 percent certain. Thus, someone might think that there are no uncaused events (every event has a cause), but he might think that there are different ways the future could turn out, since some causes are such that their effects may or may not happen. The notion of non-deterministic causes will be discussed in Chapter 5 (when we talk about **event–causal libertarianism**). Or, someone might think that every event has a cause, but that some of these causes are not part of the law-governed chain of events. For example, perhaps an agent (i.e. a *person*) can cause an event without having been determined to do so by a prior event. This means that the future is not fixed because agents can start new causal chains of events without leaving any events uncaused.

For these reasons then, we should distinguish determinism from the Principle of Universal Causation.

IS THE UNIVERSE DETERMINISTIC?

Philosophers have long disagreed about whether this kind of determinism is true. Today, many philosophers think this is a question to be answered by physicists and other scientists. In recent years, many scientists have held that determinism is false because they have noticed that quantum-level phenomena do not appear to be deterministic. In other words, on the very very very small scale, particles do not behave in entirely predictable ways. Many scientists think that our failure to predict their behavior is not just due to our lack of information, but is instead due to these particles not having set paths. Furthermore, there are processes in nature that seem not to be causally determined, such as the decay of radioactive material. Scientists can make an educated guess about how much of a radioactive substance will decay over a certain amount of time, but they can't have complete certainty (they can assign a probability). And they cannot predict when a particular atom of this substance will decay. There seems to be a measure of randomness involved. Thus, according to these scientists, the laws of nature do not fix a unique future, but they do tell us a lot about what will most likely happen. Other philosophers wonder if scientists will come back to determinism with future research and further information about how things work on the quantum level. And many philosophers think that even if quantum-level phenomena are unpredictable, that does not mean that things on the "macro level" – the big things like human beings – are not essentially determined.

It is important to note here that even those who think that determinism is false, need not deny that some things are determined. If we understand determinism, roughly, as the idea that everything is determined, to deny this is to say that *not everything is determined*. Some things can still be determined. Thus, the denial of determinism is not the same as saying that nothing is determined.

DIFFERENT KINDS OF DETERMINISM

Thus far, we have been focusing on nomological and/or causal determinism. And most of our subsequent discussions in this book will center on this kind of determinism.

But it is worth noting that there are other kinds of determinism discussed by philosophers. Sometimes philosophers discuss **logical determinism**. This kind of determinism is based on the idea that every proposition about the future is already true or false. For example, suppose I say:

I will go to the store tomorrow.

It seems that as I'm typing this today, the proposition expressed by "I will go to the store tomorrow" is true or it is false. There does not seem to be a third alternative. But that means that today, it already has the truth value that it has (i.e. true, or false). And propositions cannot change their truth values (note: if I say three days from now, "I will go to the store tomorrow", this expresses a different proposition from the one expressed by my statement today, in part because "tomorrow" refers to a different day). They have the values that they have. But if it's true today that I will go to the store tomorrow, then I will definitely go to the store tomorrow. It is already determined that I will. Notice that with logical determinism, we are not talking about causes or laws of nature. Instead, it has to do with the truth values of propositions about the future. If they have their truth values right now, then it seems that it is already fixed what I will do. Sometimes this kind of idea is called **logical fatalism**.

Another kind of determinism, **theological determinism (or theological fatalism)**, concerns **divine foreknowledge**. If God exists and has complete and infallible foreknowledge about what we will do in the future, then it seems that we are determined to do what we do. Suppose God knows today that I will choose to wear my red sweater to work next Tuesday. That means that when next Tuesday rolls around, I must choose to wear my red sweater. This is not because I have any awareness of God's foreknowledge. It's not because God is forcing me to choose the red sweater. It's not even that God's knowledge causes my choice. So why must I wear it?

Here's the problem: suppose I were to do something other than choose to wear the red sweater like God thought I would. Suppose I choose a blue shirt instead. What, then, do we say about what God knew today? Was God wrong? Did I make his belief incorrect by choosing a different shirt? This does not seem like something I should be able to do. God can't be wrong. And I don't have the power to change this about Him. Should we say that if God's knowledge is infallible then somehow it changes with my choice? But that seems to make me able to retroactively cause God to believe something else. In other words, it seems like, as I choose the blue shirt, I am somehow effecting the past – namely, God's belief from the day before. How can I do that? Again, the problem is not that God causes what I do, it's that God's infallible foreknowledge seems to make it impossible for me to do otherwise.

There are lots of interesting attempts to solve the puzzles concerning logical and theological determinism, along with some interesting attempts to say they are irresolvable. We can't get into all the details of these arguments, but I encourage those who are interested to pursue further reading on these topics (there are some suggestions at the end of this chapter).

COMPATIBILISM

Now that we have a rough idea of compatibility and incompatibility as well as of determinism, it's time to talk about compatibilism concerning free will and (causal or nomological) determinism.

As discussed earlier, compatibilism is a thesis about the relationship between free will and determinism. Compatibilists think these two things can go together – i.e. the following statements can both be true together:

(a) Human agents sometimes have free will.
(b) Our universe operates according to determinism.

Much more will be said about different compatibilist proposals in later chapters. But the central idea behind compatibilism is that the truth of determinism would not rule out free will. If determinism is true, the future is fixed. But the compatibilist does not see this as a threat to free will.

Students coming to this theory for the first time often have an urge to suppose that what the compatibilist *really* means is that we could have free will even if *almost* everything were determined, so long as our choices were not. But this is to radically misunderstand the compatibilist. The compatibilist is really saying that *even if absolutely everything were determined*, including everything we think, choose, feel, and do, we can still sometimes be free. To say that almost everything is determined is not really determinism. The compatibilist thinks that full-fledged, real determinism is not a threat to free will.

This might seem counterintuitive or incredible. How could I be free, if my desires, beliefs, thoughts, and decisions were all preordained by a causal chain starting years before my birth? But the compatibilist has a lot of compelling and intuitive reasons on his side. Some of these will be discussed shortly. And some of these reasons will come out more fully when we look at different compatibilist proposals in subsequent chapters.

SOFT DETERMINISM

As has been mentioned several times, compatibilism on its own is not a theory about whether free will exists or determinism is true. But often in the philosophical literature, compatibilism is combined with a stance on the existence of free will and/or determinism.

For example, **soft determinism** refers to a compatibilist view that holds that determinism is true and we do have free will. It will later be contrasted with an incompatibilist view called **hard determinism** (the theory that determinism is true and we do not have free will).

The soft determinist thinks there are strong reasons to believe that the world operates deterministically. But she also thinks that this does not detract from our ability to act freely. According to the soft determinist, once we understand what free will really is, we realize that it exists under determinism and perhaps even requires determinism (or at least requires that our behavior is determined).

Why, though, would free will be compatible with or even require determinism? At first glance, one might suppose this is some sort of philosophical trick. But it is based on some very deep-seated and plausible intuitions. This leads us into our next section.

WHY BE A COMPATIBILIST?

One of the reasons someone might be a compatibilist is because she believes that free will actually requires determinism. So, it's not just that the two things can go together, it's that free will actually needs determinism. Soft determinists often argue this way. (It is not necessarily only a soft determinist who might argue that free will requires determinism. Someone might argue this but not be a soft determinist, because she thinks determinism is false and thus thinks that we do not have free will. But most compatibilists do believe in free will.)

Philosophers who argue that free will requires determinism often bring up a worry mentioned in the first chapter. That is, if our actions were not determined, it seems that they would be a matter of chance. Chance events do not seem like free will, do they? They seem like random accidents rather than the kinds of things we ought to attribute to ourselves as agents.

Suppose, for example, that I am deliberating about whether to work on this chapter some more or whether to go watch TV. Suppose that, after much thought, I decide that it would be best to stay and work a bit longer on the chapter. As I continue to work, I pat myself on the back for being so diligent and resisting my less worthy but nonetheless strong urge to watch TV.

Now suppose that nothing determined this choice. So I'm thinking about my reasons for and against it, along with my reasons for and against the alternative. And then the choice to stay and work occurs, without being determined by those reasons or anything else. Well, it seems that the choice did not really come from me, or from my character. It was not determined by my reasons or my values or by who I am as a person. It's as if it just happened out of the blue. That, say these theorists, does not seem like freedom.

Those who think free will requires determinism, then, tend to believe that free choices and actions stem from our characters and are determined by them. On such a view, my choice to keep working would be free only if it were determined by certain things about me, such as my values, beliefs, and reasons. If choices and actions are not determined by these things, then where do they come from? If they are not determined, does that make it possible that on some occasions my desires and reasons all point in one direction and yet I just choose the alternative? Does it make it possible that although my character is such that I prefer one thing over another, I just do the thing I like less? Thus, some compatibilists are compatibilists because they think that the only way to make sense of free will and responsibility is if our actions and choices are actually determined by the right sorts of causes.

Why else might someone be a compatibilist? I'm sure there are many different reasons. But another major reason is that someone might believe that our central and deepest concerns about free will are just not subject to the threat of determinism. For example, **moral responsibility** tends to be one of our biggest concerns relating to free will. We tend to think that responsibility requires free will. Well, one kind of compatibilist view holds that judgments about moral responsibility would not really be affected by beliefs about determinism. In other words, this view suggests that our interactions with others and our feelings towards them would not change if we were to be convinced of the truth of determinism. We would still feel resentment towards those who have wronged us and gratitude towards those who have helped us. We would still praise and blame others based on what they do. Some philosophers extend this beyond moral responsibility. So come what may from the world of science, these philosophers suggest that the truth of determinism does not affect whether I am the author of my actions, or whether I can express my individuality the way I want to. On the practical side, one might prefer compatibilism because one need not abandon one's belief in freedom in the event that scientists come to a consensus that determinism is definitively true.

Incompatibilists often argue that moral responsibility requires that one could have avoided what one did and they argue that if determinism is true, no one could have avoided anything. This will be discussed in a later chapter, but it should be noted here that some philosophers are compatibilists (at least with respect to the kind of free will required for moral responsibility) because they think that the incompatibilists are wrong about this. These compatibilists think there are examples that prove that our intuitions about moral responsibility are not based on the idea that the agent could have avoided what he did.

INCOMPATIBILISM

As we've already noted, incompatibilism is the view that free will and determinism cannot go together. But as noted earlier, just saying you are an incompatibilist does not tell me whether you think we have free will, or whether you think determinism is true. Perhaps you think we lack free will and determinism is true. Or perhaps you think we have free will and determinism is false. Or perhaps you think we lack free will and determinism is false. But what you've ruled out is that we have free will and determinism is true.

LIBERTARIANISM

In the context of the free will debate, **libertarianism** means something a bit different from the way it is often used. It's not a political position. Obviously, the words have similar origins relating to the idea of "liberty", but the libertarian about free will is not called this due to a particular political ideology. The word instead refers to a kind of incompatibilist. A libertarian is an incompatibilist who believes that we have free will. That means the libertarian must also believe that determinism is false.

In a later chapter we will consider a few different kinds of libertarian views. Roughly speaking, there are three general categories. Some libertarians argue that our free actions are uncaused. This is sometimes called **simple indeterminism**. Other libertarians argue that our free actions are caused by appropriate mental events. But they argue that because these causes are not deterministic, our actions can still be free. These libertarians are often called event-causal libertarians. A third kind of libertarian view is called **agent causation**. Agent-causal theorists argue that our free actions are not caused by mental events but are caused by agents (i.e. persons). All three views will be discussed in more detail later.

HARD DETERMINISM AND HARD INCOMPATIBILISM

Some incompatibilists think that determinism is true so we therefore do not have free will. These incompatibilists are called hard determinists. Hard determinists agree with libertarians that free will requires that our free actions are not determined. But since they believe that determinism is true, they think free will cannot exist.

In recent years, some philosophers have also argued for something called **hard incompatibilism**. Those who believe in this view agree with hard determinists in thinking that we do not have free will. They agree with both libertarians and hard determinists in thinking that free will is incompatible with determinism. But they also think that a lack of determinism (i.e. **indeterminism**) would not allow for free will either. In other words, hard incompatibilists think that free will does not go together with determinism or indeterminism. They think it does not go with determinism for reasons that will be spelled out in the next section. But they think that it does not go with indeterminism for the same reasons that were mentioned above when discussing the worries about the randomness of undetermined actions. Unlike the hard determinist, the hard incompatibilist may not have a definite view on whether determinism is true. He just thinks that, either way, we wouldn't have free will.

WHY BE AN INCOMPATIBILIST?

You may already have some thoughts about why someone would be an incompatibilist. Perhaps the statement of determinism above is enough to make you think that this would clearly rule out free will. But compatibilist intuitions cannot be dismissed so easily. Compatibilists have a lot of good reasons for thinking that the kind of free will we care about is not undermined by determinism. And they have some good reasons for worrying that undetermined action is possibly more problematic. So incompatibilists need some reasons behind their view.

One reason incompatibilists often give for their view is something called the **Principle of Alternative (or Alternate) Possibilities (PAP)**. It is often stated in terms of moral responsibility, but some philosophers also put it in terms of free will.

PAP: A person acted freely (or morally responsibly) only if he could have done otherwise.

This principle seems fairly intuitive. In fact, it is so intuitive that folks on both sides of the debate (i.e. incompatibilists and compatibilists) have often assumed it to be true. But incompatibilists sometimes try to argue that it is only their view that makes any sense out of the principle.

Why is the principle so intuitive? Well, we tend to think that free actions are those we could have avoided performing. For example, we tend to think that Joe freely knocked Ken over if he could have avoided knocking him over. He could have done something else, i.e. "could have done otherwise". Joe could have stayed still, or walked around Ken, or sat down, or whatever. Unfree actions, on the other hand, seem to be those that we could not have avoided. There was no way to have done anything other than what we did do. Perhaps someone pushed Joe into Ken so that Joe really couldn't have avoided knocking Ken over. In this case, we would probably say that Joe didn't freely knock Ken down and we would probably say that it wasn't Joe's fault. This is because we tend to think it problematic or even unfair to hold someone morally responsible for something he could not have avoided. It is often a way of excusing someone to say, "but he could not have helped it. He had to do it. It could not have been avoided. He could not have done otherwise."

Why do incompatibilists think that only their position makes any sense out of the principle? Incompatibilists often argue that if determinism is true, then no one could have ever acted otherwise than he in fact acted. After all, if it was predetermined from the "Big Bang" that I would be typing this sentence, then how can anyone say I could have done otherwise than to type it when I did? We will see later that some compatibilists will say that there is an important way of understanding "could" that allows us to say that on many occasions I could have done otherwise, even if determinism is true. But incompatibilists suggest that, in the way we care about when it comes to free will, it does not make sense to say I *ever* could have done otherwise if determinism is true. If determinism is true, then there is only one way that things will go. How, then, could anyone ever do otherwise?

Another kind of reasoning for incompatibilism is based on something that is called the **Consequence Argument**. The basic idea goes like this. Determinism says that what I do is necessitated by the past and the laws of nature. But I don't have any control over the past and the laws of nature. I can't be held responsible for them either. How, then, can I have the right sort of control over what I do since what I do necessarily follows from things that I don't control? Suppose I scratch my nose at a particular time. My nose-scratching is supposedly the inevitable result of the past and the laws of nature, if determinism is true. In order to avoid scratching my nose at that moment, I would have to change the past (change the events that led up to it) or I would have to break a law of nature. I do not have control over either of these things. Thus, I don't have control over my nose-scratching.

SUMMARY AND CONCLUSION

So we've seen that there is a big debate between those who think that free will and determinism are compatible and those who do not. Within these two categories, there are lots of positions concerning whether we have free will or whether determinism is true.

The following table summarizes the major positions discussed in this chapter:

Table 2.1 Major positions in the debate

Incompatibilism	Free Will	Determinism
Libertarianism:	Yes	No
Simple Indeterminism	Yes	No
Event-causal Libertarianism	Yes	No
Agent-causal Libertarianism	Yes	No
Hard Determinism	No	Yes
Hard Incompatibilism	No	It doesn't matter. We do not have the kind of free will required for responsibility in any case.

Compatibilism	Free Will	Determinism
Soft Determinism	Yes	Yes
Other Compatibilisms	Yes	It doesn't matter for the kind of freedom required for responsibility

There are lots of good reasons for each position. We will examine some of these reasons in the chapters to come. One way you might look at the debate between compatibilists and incompatibilists is as a debate over what kind of freedom we think we need or want. Clearly, free will is going to be characterized differently depending on one's intuitions about compatibility. How do we decide? Maybe it comes down to the kind of freedom that we think is worthwhile. What kind of freedom do we want? What kind do we need in order to be the responsible, creative, and autonomous beings that we think we are?

FURTHER READING

For an accurate and thorough general overview of determinism, see: Carl Hoefer, "Causal Determinism", in Edward N. Zalta (ed.), *The Stanford Encyclopedia of Philosophy* (Winter 2008 Edition), www.plato.stanford.edu/archives/win2008/entries/determinism-causal.

On logical determinism or logical fatalism, see Richard Taylor, "Fatalism", *Philosophical Review,* 71(1) (1962): 56–66; and Richard Taylor, "Fate", in *Metaphysics*, 4th edition (Englewood Cliffs, NJ: Prentice Hall, 1991). The latter is particularly accessible and lively.

For an important and famous treatment of the dilemma of freedom and God's foreknowledge, see Nelson Pike, "Divine Omniscience and Voluntary Action", *Philosophical Review*, 74(1) (1965): 27–46.

Two excellent books on the problem of theological fatalism are: John Martin Fischer (ed.), *God, Foreknowledge and Freedom* (Stanford, CA: Stanford University Press, 1989); and Linda Trinkaus Zagzebski, *The Dilemma of Freedom and Foreknowledge* (Oxford: Oxford University Press, 1991).

For a thorough and accurate overview of arguments for incompatibilism, see: Kadri Vihvelin, "Arguments for Incompatibilism", in Edward N. Zalta (ed.), *The Stanford Encyclopedia of Philosophy* (Fall 2008 Edition), www.plato.stanford.edu/archives/fall2008/entries/incompatibilism-arguments.

For the famous Consequence Argument (along with other important issues relating to free will and incompatibilism), see Peter van Inwagen, *An Essay on Free Will* (Oxford: Clarendon Press, 1983).

For a good overview on laws of nature, see John W. Carroll, "Laws of Nature", in Edward N. Zalta (ed.), *The Stanford Encyclopedia of Philosophy* (Spring 2012 Edition), www.plato.stanford.edu/archives/spr2012/entries/laws-of-nature.

3

MORAL RESPONSIBILITY AND ALTERNATIVE POSSIBILITIES

Suppose we don't have free will? So what? Why do we care?

Again, one of the main reasons we care about whether we have free will is that we care about **moral responsibility**. We care about whether we are blameworthy or praiseworthy for our choices and actions. Most people agree that moral responsibility requires some sort of free will. It does not seem appropriate to blame or praise someone if he was not free to act as he did. But as we saw in the last chapter, there is a lot of disagreement about whether this kind of free will is compatible with **determinism**. Can we have the kind of freedom required for moral responsibility if determinism is true? What has to be true in order for someone to be morally responsible? What kind of freedom is required?

MORAL RESPONSIBILITY

Before we look at what may be required for moral responsibility, we should say a bit about what is meant by moral responsibility. There are a number of different viewpoints. For example, some philosophers have suggested that holding others responsible – that is, praising and blaming them – is just a way of modifying their behavior. On this view, blaming someone is a way of getting him to stop doing what he is doing, while praising him is a way of getting him to continue doing the kinds of things he is doing. Basically, no one likes to be censured or yelled at, and everyone likes to be the subject of adulation. On this view, blame and praise are behaviors we engage in for practical reasons so that society can run smoothly. (Notice that, on this view, it does not matter whether determinism is true. Thus, *some* compatibilists have held this view. Even if everything I do is determined, it could still make sense to blame me for the bad things that I do in order to influence my future behavior. This future behavior has already been determined, but being blamed by others could be the determined path to it.)

Other philosophers (both compatibilist and incompatibilist) do not like this model and suggest that it is not good enough. These philosophers don't deny that praise and blame influence behavior, but they think that true responsibility involves more. True responsibility involves **desert**. Does the person deserve to be praised or blamed? Suppose little Trina has been raised in an environment in which she has been taught that hurting people is what we ought to do and that it is really quite amusing. Trina aims to please. She responds well to praise and modifies her behavior when censured. Suppose that Trina goes to school for the first time. Wanting to make a good impression, she starts the day off by tripping up as many of her classmates as she can. Obviously, most of us would agree that this behavior is undesirable. But I think many of us would be inclined to think that Trina does not deserve blame for it. She does not know any better. She has been raised poorly and she is too young and inexperienced to be expected to have reflected upon the errors of her upbringing. One might believe, however, that it would be *useful* to blame Trina. It would be useful because Trina responds well to this sort of thing. This would modify her behavior for the better. If others hold her responsible and blame her, she will almost certainly be less likely to engage in this problematic behavior in the future. But there are two points we might make here. First, we might question whether it's fair to blame someone when she does not really deserve to be blamed. Clearly it can be useful to blame someone even if she does not deserve it. Second, we might distinguish between *correcting* one's behavior and blaming one for it. Those who think it unfair to blame Trina might nonetheless think it okay to correct her behavior in some gentle and reasonable way.

Thus, there seem to be at least two different notions of responsibility: A deeper, more robust notion (i.e. desert) and a shallower, less robust notion. For the sake of simplicity, I will not distinguish between these two notions in the remainder of this chapter. But you might think about them on your own and reflect upon whether one or the other goes better with the positions that are discussed.

REACTIVE ATTITUDES

Is there anything else we can say about how to characterize praise and blame? One important view of responsibility is inspired by the work of P.F. Strawson. Strawson suggests that responsibility has to do with being an appropriate target of certain natural human attitudes. These are the ways we react to one another as persons. He calls these the **reactive attitudes**. If you purposely stomp on my toes, I react to this by having certain attitudes towards you: e.g. resentment, indignation, anger, and so on. If you save my beloved dog, I also react by having certain attitudes towards you: e.g. affection, gratitude, and so forth. On this view, praise and blame are not just about the practical consequences of influencing one another's behavior (though of course they do have that effect). Instead, praise and blame are part of deep-seated human attitudes that make up who we are as persons. Furthermore, these attitudes are only appropriately directed towards other **moral agents** – that is, towards beings who are capable of undertaking and understanding moral behavior. It is not appropriate for me to resent the mosquito that bites me, or the computer that crashes as I'm writing. I may be angry in these instances, but it's not really appropriate for me to *blame* the mosquito or the computer the way I'd blame a moral agent. The latter is an appropriate target of blame (assuming the right kind of circumstances), unlike the mosquito or computer. Many, but not all, philosophers utilize something like this characterization.

MORAL AGENCY

But what does it mean to be a moral agent (like you and me, unlike the mosquito or the computer)? There are lots of things that probably have to be true of someone in order for him to be a moral agent. There is a lot of philosophical literature on this issue, but suffice it to say that most philosophers agree that **moral agency** at least requires certain cognitive abilities. Dogs, cats, and very young children, for example, while clearly agents with desires, motives, and so forth, probably do not qualify as moral agents because they lack certain intellectual capacities. This does not, of course, mean that animals and children are morally irrelevant. In fact, our treatment of such beings is highly morally relevant (for example, many people argue that it is morally wrong to be unnecessarily cruel to animals). It just means that these beings do not have all the capacities they would need to have in order to be morally blameworthy and praiseworthy for what they do. Exactly which capabilities they are lacking is a tricky issue, but here are some possibilities: an ability to fully understand consequences of actions, an ability to evaluate their own motives and desires, an ability to see others as full-fledged agents with their own purposes, and an ability to see themselves as moral agents. A human baby is not automatically a moral agent, but develops into one if all goes as it should.

This means that most human adults (those with the requisite capabilities) are moral agents who can appropriately be blamed and praised for what they do. But this is far from the end of the story. The question now is *when* (upon which occasions) moral agents can be held responsible. It is highly implausible to suppose that once someone becomes a moral agent, she is thereafter responsible for everything she does, regardless of the circumstances. I am a moral agent, but I do not think that I can be fairly blamed for everything that I do. But why not? Why are there some things I do for which I am not deserving of blame? Which actions are those that one can be blamed for and which are not? What conditions must be present or absent in order to blame and praise? (Some philosophers argue that no one is ever responsible, but we will come back to that view later.) Thus, moral agents are those who can be appropriately held responsible, but only when the conditions are right.

THE PRINCIPLE OF ALTERNATIVE POSSIBILITIES (PAP)

When are the conditions right for responsibility? We can't get into all of the conditions here, but we can look at some important suggestions about what is required for moral responsibility or what rules it out.

As we saw in the last chapter, some people think that responsibility is always absent if determinism is true. Thus, one condition, according to these philosophers (incompatibilists) is that determinism must be false. Others (compatibilists) think that determinism need not undermine responsibility. Note that compatibilists do not think that agents are always responsible (there are other conditions that must be satisfied). They just think that the absence of determinism is not one of the conditions for responsibility.

But it doesn't really help us to just try to decide whether the absence of determinism is or is not a condition. It does not tell us why responsibility can or cannot be present if determinism is true. Why does one side think so and the other does not? So, what we should do is think about the conditions of responsibility more generally. What do our intuitions tell us about responsibility? If determinism takes away responsibility, what is it about determinism that has this consequence?

Coming up with conditions for responsibility is a harder task than it might seem, and there will probably never be a complete consensus amongst philosophers. But one way to proceed is to look at fairly uncontroversial cases in which responsibility seems to be absent. This may not give us a full set of conditions for responsibility, but it might tell us something important about what responsibility seems to require.

EXCUSING CONDITIONS

When responsibility is absent, we often think in terms of excusing conditions. We all make excuses from time to time. This is a pretty common human practice. Excuses serve to get us off the hook for something we have done.

> "The devil made me do it."
> "What other choice did I have?"
> "It was unavoidable."
> "She pushed me."
> "I didn't see you there."
> "I didn't know the gun was loaded."

Excuses come in different shapes and sizes. Even as long ago as Aristotle (384–322 BCE), philosophers tried to come up with the kinds of conditions that prevent us from being blameworthy. In other words, what kinds of excuses are effective (assuming we are taken at our word)? Aristotle suggests, roughly, that we are not responsible when something is not done voluntarily. And it is not done voluntarily if it is the result of force or certain kinds of ignorance. For our purposes here, the notion of force is more relevant. (For those who are curious about ignorance, I will point out that the last two excuses on the above list are classic cases of responsibility-undermining ignorance. Another good example of responsibility-undermining ignorance is the case of Oedipus. He cannot be blamed for marrying his mother (i.e. committing incest), because he did not know that Jocasta was his mother. While what an agent knows is certainly relevant to his responsibility, for our purposes, we will set these kinds of cases aside.)

For Aristotle, force has to do with whether the action originated outside the agent and the agent did not contribute to it (i.e. he did not choose it). For example, suppose the wind knocks me into you and you fall over. I am not to blame for knocking you over because I did not choose to – it is the wind, not me, that is to blame. The absence of force seems like a plausible condition for responsibility. Of course, much more would have to be said about what counts as force. What does it mean for an agent to contribute to the action? What does it mean for the action to originate outside the agent (more will be said about some of these things later).

More recently, philosophers writing about free will and its connection to responsibility have focused on whether the agent "could have done otherwise". If not, the agent does not seem to be responsible. The basic idea is that it does not seem appropriate to blame someone if there was nothing else he could have done. If the action was unavoidable, how is it fair to blame him? Thus, excuses like, "it was unavoidable" or "there was no other choice" serve to get agents off the hook.

WHAT IS THE PRINCIPLE OF ALTERNATIVE POSSIBILITIES (PAP)?

This brings us to the famous **Principle of Alternative (or Alternate) Possibilities (PAP)**:

> PAP: A person acted freely (and morally responsibly) only if she could have done otherwise.

The Principle of Alternative Possibilities is intuitively plausible. And many philosophers still believe that it is true. But, as we shall see, many other philosophers think that it is false. Before we get to that, however, let's look at the principle more closely and see how those on different sides of the debate have utilized it.

Very generally, when we say that someone "could have done otherwise", we are looking at someone's action and saying that she had the ability to do something else instead. Suppose I went for a walk yesterday. Could I have done otherwise? Could I have stayed home to write? Or gone out for coffee? Or gone jogging? Or done nothing? To say that I could have done otherwise is just to say that although I did in fact go for a walk, going for that walk was not unavoidable. This seems very straightforward. But how can we tell whether someone had the ability to do something different? What does it mean to say I *could have* done such and such? What kind of ability is at issue here?

THE CONDITIONAL ANALYSIS OF "COULD HAVE DONE OTHERWISE"

Philosophers have analyzed "could have" in different ways. One way of looking at it is that when we say "could have" there is a hidden "if". In other words, "could have" is really "*would have, if* ... " And the "if" is filled in with certain conditions, depending on context. I could have done better on the exam means something like, "I would have done better if I had studied more". I could have been a gladiator means, "I would have been a gladiator if I had lived in ancient Rome" (and various other conditions were fulfilled). I could have made that shot: "I would have made that shot if ... you hadn't bumped me. If ... I had practiced more. If ... I had been concentrating better. If ... I had any skill whatsoever!"

In the free will context, some philosophers have filled in this "if" with the choices, or efforts, or desires of the agent. I "could have" becomes "I would have, if I had chosen to ... " or " ... if I had tried" or " ... if I had wanted to". Let's call this the **Conditional Analysis**. Notice that the "if" clause is filled in with the choices or efforts or desires of the person acting. Suppose I knock you over. You want to know whether to blame me, so you want to know whether I could have done otherwise. According to the Conditional Analysis, I could have done otherwise means that I would have done otherwise than to knock you over had I chosen to do otherwise than to knock you over. Suppose I decided to knock you over because I wanted to get ahead of you in line. To suggest that I could have done otherwise would be to suggest that had I chosen to do something other than knock you over, I would have done something other than to knock you over. Thus, I can be blamed for knocking you down.

Here is the key to understanding the Conditional Analysis: *if my own choice (or desire or effort) was what prevented me from doing otherwise*, then (according to its proponents) I was not really forced into doing what I did. I did it of my own free will.

But now let's change the example. Suppose that instead of my knocking you over because I want to get ahead in line, someone slammed into me, causing me to slam into you and knock you over. Then it seems plausible to suggest that even if I had chosen to do otherwise, I would have knocked you over anyway. Thus, I would not have done otherwise had I chosen otherwise. I really had no say in the matter and so I can't be held responsible. In other words, my choice (or desire or effort) was not what prevented me from doing otherwise.

So, on the Conditional Analysis, the Principle of Alternative Possibilities tells us that I am responsible in the first case and not in the second. On this view, something is considered to be avoidable in the relevant way so long as it depends on my choice or my effort. If I would have avoided the action had I tried, or had I chosen to do so, then it's sufficiently avoidable and it's fair to blame me for it.

Historically, some important philosophers have advocated this kind of analysis in line with compatibilism. Recall that the compatibilist believes that free will (the kind required for responsibility) is not threatened by determinism. Some compatibilists like this analysis because it allows them to maintain the Principle of Alternative Possibilities (a plausible principle) and supposedly show that one "could have done otherwise" even under determinism.

For example, suppose I ate cereal this morning for breakfast. Suppose that determinism is true and therefore I was causally determined to eat cereal this morning (the past and the laws of nature guaranteed that I would eat just the cereal I did in fact eat at just the time I ate it). At first, it seems impossible to suppose that I could have done otherwise. If I was determined by the past and the laws of nature to eat cereal, how does it make any sense to say that I could have, say, eaten toast, or skipped breakfast? And at first it seems as if the compatibilist is in trouble. If the Principle of Alternative Possibilities is true and freedom (and responsibility) requires being able to do otherwise, then it seems as if determinism does rule out the kind of freedom associated with responsibility.

But historically, some important compatibilists argued that if "could have" is understood in the conditional way we just discussed, then it is not at all impossible to suppose that I could have done otherwise, *even if I were determined*. Take the cereal example. Assume that there was nothing strange about my action. Suppose I deliberated about what I wanted to eat, I chose what I wanted to eat, and I went through the normal motions of getting myself a bowl of cereal. This is all consistent with determinism. It's just that under determinism, all my thought processes and deliberations and desires are part of the deterministic causal chain. Some compatibilists suggest that although it seems as if I couldn't have done anything but eat cereal, there's a sense in which I *could have* had toast. I *would have* had toast had I *chosen* to eat toast. It just so happens that the deterministic chain did not have me choosing toast.

On this analysis, the compatibilist is suggesting that so long as no constraining factors are coming between the agent's wants or choices and the agent's action, the agent is acting freely (assuming any other relevant conditions have been fulfilled). In other words, the kind of free will required for responsibility does not rely on the absence of determinism. It relies on the absence of these constraining factors. For these philosophers, free will means being able to do what one wants, chooses, or tries to do. So, for example, if someone had tied me up and force-fed me cereal, then it would make sense to say that I could not have done otherwise than to eat cereal. I would not have done otherwise even if I had chosen. Once again, the difference is that when I am free, it is my own choice or efforts or desires that prevent me from doing otherwise. When I am not free, on the other hand, my inability to do otherwise does not depend on these things, but depends upon constraining factors.

For the compatibilist, determinism is not enough to take away freedom and responsibility. On the Conditional Analysis, this is because determinism does not mean that one could not have done otherwise. If the action followed in the right way from one's wants and choices, then there was sufficient freedom. If the action followed from one's choices, then that seems to indicate that a different choice would have resulted in a different action. Thus, one would have done differently had one chosen differently.

Classical (or traditional) compatibilism refers to a kind of compatibilism espoused in the seventeenth and eighteenth centuries (by philosophers such as Hobbes and Hume) and again in the twentieth century. Classical compatibilists defined free will as an agent's unhindered ability to do what he wants. Determinism does not take away our ability to do what we want. For all we know, determinism has always been true. Haven't you been able to do what you wanted on many occasions? On their view, determinism does not hinder us. This is because we are often able to act on our wishes without anything standing in the way. We are not in chains, in prison, or otherwise compelled to act against our own wishes.

Because of the plausibility of the Principle of Alternative Possibilities (that freedom and responsibility requires being able to do otherwise), many classical compatibilists utilized the Conditional Analysis of "could have done otherwise". (Not all of them did so. Hobbes, for example, did not utilize the Conditional Analysis.) They suggested that if one acted on one's wishes unhindered (as their view of freedom requires) then one could have done otherwise even under determinism. This is because one would have acted otherwise had one wished to.

PROBLEMS FOR THE CONDITIONAL ANALYSIS

But unfortunately for these classical compatibilists, the Conditional Analysis has met with serious and perhaps fatal objections. Take the cereal example again. The Conditional Analysis suggests that so long as I would have avoided cereal had I chosen to, or tried to, or wanted to (and, for example, chosen toast or eggs or nothing), then I am free in eating the cereal. Different wants would have led to a different action, so I am not being forced into something in spite of what I want. But is this good enough? Don't we need to know whether I could have avoided wanting cereal? In other words, if my desire for cereal is forced upon me, doesn't this take away my freedom even though I am not being forced into acting against a desire? What if it is not really up to me whether I want cereal?

Then how am I free, even though I pour it into the bowl because I want it? The Conditional Analysis makes it look as if all that matters is whether I am able to act on what I want. But if I can't help what I want, then it seems that I really don't have any alternative even though the Conditional Analysis says that I do. If I have to want cereal and I choose and act based on what I want, then how can I really do otherwise? Yes, even if I can't help what I want it can be true that I would have done something different had I wanted to. It's just that I could not have wanted to.

The problem for the Conditional Analysis is that it gives the wrong results. It says that we have an alternative even when we don't. It says that even if I can't help wanting cereal, I can still do otherwise than to eat it. But this may not be true. If my actions follow from my wants and I do not control my wants, then how can I do otherwise?

Though there are some recent interesting attempts to give a compatibilist analysis of "could have done otherwise", it seems that the compatibilist has some work to do in convincing us that a plausible analysis can be given. But this does not mean that the compatibilist project has failed. As we will see later, the compatibilist has some other maneuvers.

The incompatibilist, however, seems to have the upper hand at this point, since he argues that the Principle of Alternative Possibilities is plausible and claims that determinism would rule out the ability to do otherwise. The incompatibilist suggests that it's not really an ability to do otherwise unless right at the time of action (or decision), even had everything been the same leading up to that point, the agent could have done otherwise. In other words, it's not that the agent would have done something different had something prior to the action been different (such as his wishes, choice, or effort). Instead, it's that even had everything been the same, he could have done something else.

FRANKFURT-STYLE COUNTEREXAMPLES TO THE PRINCIPLE OF ALTERNATIVE POSSIBILITIES

But is the Principle of Alternative Possibilities true? It seems plausible enough, but maybe it does not really hold up as a principle. This is just what some philosophers have argued. They give counterexamples to the principle to show that it does not hold up. A **counter-example** is a scenario (often fictional, sometimes quite fanciful) that disproves a rule. It illustrates a case in which the rule does not hold. The Principle of Alternative Possibilities says that a person is responsible/free *only if* she could have done otherwise. This means that to disprove the rule, someone can give an example in which a person is responsible but could not have done otherwise. Thus, it's not *only* if able to do otherwise that a person is responsible. There might be occasions on which a person is responsible anyway. Maybe these aren't the usual cases, but even one counterexample is enough. The principle is supposed to hold in general. It is supposed to tell us what has to be true in order for someone to be responsible. It says that there had to have been an alternative. If there is a scenario in which our intuitions tell us that a person is responsible without having alternatives, then the principle does not generally hold.

Counterexamples to the Principle of Alternative Possibilities seem to be inspired by an example that comes from philosopher John Locke (1632–1704). Locke gives the example of a man who, while asleep, is carried into a room where he finds someone he is happy to see and talk with. Unbeknownst to him, the door to the room is locked. But the man stays willingly in the room since he is happy to find himself there. We can say that the man is responsible for staying in the room, even though he could not have done otherwise. Some will say that the man could in fact have done otherwise because he could have chosen to try to leave. He could have struggled with the door or tried to call someone to open it, or what have you. If the man could in fact have done otherwise, then it seems that this example does not disprove the Principle of Alternative Possibilities. It does not give a case in which someone is responsible even though he could not have done otherwise. The man in this case is responsible, but perhaps he could have done otherwise in the sense that he could have chosen otherwise.

In the twentieth century, philosopher Harry Frankfurt revitalized this sort of example and modified it. The modifications allow it to get around the above issue. Furthermore, many philosophers since Frankfurt have given variations of these examples. They have come to be called **Frankfurt-style counterexamples** to the Principle of Alternative Possibilities. Here is a very basic Frankfurt-style counter-example: Suppose Kathy wants to kill Virginia. Suppose that Ned really wants Kathy to kill Virginia, but he doesn't want to get involved if he does not have to. So Ned figures out a way to make Kathy kill Virginia (in some examples this kind of character is an evil neurosurgeon who can manipulate the brain of his "victim"), but only if Kathy does not decide to do so on her own. In other words, Ned will not get involved at all, unless it looks to him as if Kathy is going to chicken out (we are to suppose that Ned has a way of telling what Kathy is going to decide to do – either because she has a sort of "tell" or perhaps because he has secretly implanted something in her brain that lets him know). We are asked to suppose that Kathy kills Virginia on her own, without Ned having to get involved. But because Ned was standing by, ready to make Kathy do it, she was unable to do otherwise. No matter what, she was going to kill Virginia. As it happens, she killed Virginia on her own. Thus, it seems that we should think Kathy is blameworthy for killing Virginia. After all, she did it on her own and because she wanted to. The fact that she couldn't have done otherwise does not seem to matter. We still blame her for what she did. If this is right, then the Principle of Alternative Possibilities appears to be false. In other words, it's not the ability to do otherwise that is required for responsibility. If this were required, then we'd think Kathy was not blameworthy (since she couldn't have done otherwise). So it seems that blame and praise are based on something else, not on an ability to do otherwise.

Frankfurt started a huge debate, one that is ongoing. An enormous number of articles have been written on these kinds of examples. Some philosophers think that these examples are decisive. They think that the Principle of Alternative Possibilities must be false because of them. Other philosophers (those who still believe in the Principle of Alternative Possibilities) suggest that the counterexamples do not work for various reasons. Some defenders of the Principle of Alternative Possibilities claim that these supposed "counterexamples" are not really counterexamples after all. Here is their reasoning. They agree that these examples are examples in which we blame the agent. Our intuitions do tell us that Kathy is blameworthy and this seems correct. But contrary to initial appearances, Kathy does in fact have an alternative in this example. The Principle of Alternative Possibilities therefore still holds. In other words, we do not have a case of responsibility without alternatives. We have a more complicated case of responsibility with an alternative. But how does Kathy have an alternative? Doesn't Ned guarantee that she has no alternative – that she must kill Virginia? And can't the person constructing the example tell the story however he likes? Some defenders of the principle, though, suggest that although Kathy does not have the alternatives of "kill Virginia" or "do not kill Virginia", she does have the alternatives of "kill Virginia on my own" or "kill Virginia as the result of Ned's manipulation". Thus, says this line of reasoning, Kathy does have an alternative and she is responsible.

It is difficult to decide who is correct – the defender of the principle or the defender of the Frankfurt-style counterexample. It does in fact seem as if there is a difference between doing something on one's own and doing it as the result of some manipulator. But, as philosopher John Fischer suggests, it also seems as if this "flicker of freedom" is not really the robust kind of alternative that would explain why someone is responsible. In other words, the person defending the Principle of Alternative Possibilities is suggesting that responsibility rests on the existence of alternatives. Shouldn't these alternatives be robust and not just amount to the difference between doing something on one's own and doing it as the result of someone's intervention? (There is a lot of disagreement on how to answer this question.)

There are other arguments offered on both sides, but I will leave those to the interested reader to pursue. There are some suggestions at the end of this chapter.

WHAT'S AT STAKE?

Why do these arguments over the Principle of Alternative Possibilities and counterexamples matter for the free will debate? Suppose the counterexamples work (and thus, the principle is false). So what? Recall that some compatibilists (some of the classical compatibilists for example) try to give a conditional analysis of "could have done otherwise". They say that "could have ... " means "would have, if I had chosen otherwise (or had tried to do otherwise and so on)". But we saw that this analysis has major problems. It seems to give the wrong result. Even if I would have done otherwise had I chosen otherwise, it is not necessarily the case that I could have done otherwise. As we said before, the fact that this analysis does not work does not mean that the compatibilist must give up her view. But it does give the incompatibilist the upper hand. But now we have counterexamples to the Principle of Alternative Possibilities – that is, we have examples to show that one does not have to have been able to do otherwise in order to be responsible. If that's right, then perhaps the compatibilist does not even need to bother with giving an analysis of "could have done otherwise". "Could have done otherwise" becomes irrelevant.

Although not all philosophers agree that these counterexamples are successful, their persuasiveness has been seen as something of a victory for compatibilism. If it's irrelevant whether someone could have done otherwise, then perhaps it's irrelevant whether determinism is true. The compatibilist need not worry about giving an analysis of "could have done otherwise". He can look elsewhere for the conditions of moral responsibility and the kind of freedom it requires.

John Fischer has coined the term **semi-compatibilism** to refer to a two-part view relating to these issues. The first part says that determinism is most likely incompatible with the ability to do otherwise. In other words, if determinism is true, the semi-compatibilist thinks that it could very well be true that we are not able to do otherwise (as the incompatibilist suggests). If everything proceeds in a deterministic causal chain, then perhaps there is not really a legitimate sense in which someone had an alternative at the time of action. But the second part of the view goes against the incompatibilists. The second part of the view is that even though determinism rules out the ability to do otherwise, it does not rule out the kind of freedom required for moral responsibility. Now that we've looked at Frankfurt-style counterexamples we see why someone might think that determinism need not rule out the freedom required for responsibility: it need not since moral responsibility does not require the ability to do otherwise. The view is *semi*-compatibilist because of the incompatibility between determinism and the ability to do otherwise.

SOURCE INCOMPATIBILISM

As we have seen, it seems that compatibilists have a vested interest in the success of Frankfurt-style counterexamples. If these examples work, then the Principle of Alternative Possibilities is false and the incompatibilist cannot use the principle against the compatibilist. But even if the Principle of Alternative Possibilities is false, that doesn't mean that the incompatibilist loses. Some incompatibilists argue that determinism rules out responsibility for reasons other than ruling out alternatives. In other words, even if we don't need alternatives in order to be responsible, this doesn't mean that determinism is no threat. Determinism may take away more than alternatives. But what does it take away? According to many incompatibilists, determinism takes away one's ability to be the ultimate source of one's action.

What does it mean to be the source of one's action? Being the source of one's action means that the action comes from the agent in the appropriate way. Perhaps this is something like Aristotle's claim (discussed earlier) that the agent contributes to the action. If the wind just pushes me into someone, I am not really the source of this motion. My body is involved of course, but I am not engaged in an action as its source. But if I decide to push someone, I am the source of this action. I contribute by choosing to perform it and moving my body accordingly.

So far, none of this is inconsistent with determinism. I could choose to push someone over even if determinism is true. And I could be considered the source of my action because I am involved in a crucial way in the production of this event (it's just that if determinism is true, then I was predetermined to choose to push someone). In fact, many compatibilists would agree that we must be the sources of our actions in order to be responsible. But many incompatibilists insist that we must be the *ultimate* sources of our actions. And determinism does purportedly rule out this ability.

What does it mean to be the ultimate source of one's action? Being the ultimate source means that the action originates in the agent. It's not just that the agent contributes to the action. It's that nothing outside of the agent guarantees the action. If determinism is true, the past and the laws of nature do guarantee the action. This means that the agent is not the ultimate source of her action. She may be *a* source, but not the ultimate source. Thus, my choice to push someone (if determinism is true) has been guaranteed by things outside of me – the past and the laws of nature. And this was all guaranteed long before I was born. Thus, source incompatibilists emphasize the incompatibility of determinism and ultimate sourcehood, instead of emphasizing alternative possibilities. So the falsity of the Principle of Alternative Possibilities may not matter so much to these incompatibilists. Determinism is a threat to responsibility because it threatens sourcehood.

SUMMARY

To sum up, we care about free will in large part because we care about moral responsibility. Some philosophers think that the kind of freedom required for moral responsibility is a kind that involves alternative possibilities (these philosophers believe in the Principle of Alternative Possibilities). Other philosophers think that the principle can be disproven by counterexamples (so-called "Frankfurt-style counterexamples"), or at least that alternative possibilities are not the crucial requirement for responsibility (many compatibilists as well as source incompatibilists).

Of those who believe in the Principle of Alternative Possibilities, some think that alternatives are not ruled out by determinism (for example, some classical compatibilists who give a conditional analysis of "could have done otherwise"). Others who believe in the Principle of Alternative Possibilities think that alternatives are ruled out by determinism (many incompatibilists). Then there is the semi-compatibilist who does not believe in the Principle of Alternative Possibilities but also believes that determinism rules out alternatives.

Here is a summary of some of the positions we have discussed in this chapter:

Traditional incompatibilism: The Principle of Alternative Possibilities is true. Determinism threatens free will/responsibility because it rules out alternatives.

Source incompatibilism: Determinism threatens free will because it rules out the ability of an agent to be the ultimate source of her actions. The existence of alternatives is not the issue. The Principle of Alternative Possibilities could be false and Frankfurt-style counterexamples to it could be successful. But determinism is still a threat.

Classical compatibilism: Free will is the unhindered ability to do what one wants. Determinism does not rule this out. This view is often paired with:

Conditional Analysis: The Principle of Alternative Possibilities is true. But "could have done otherwise" means "would have if I had chosen to, tried to, or wanted to". Thus determinism does not threaten free will because it does not conflict with this understanding of "could have done otherwise".

Other compatibilisms: The Principle of Alternative Possibilities is false. Frankfurt-style counterexamples prove that one can be free in the way required for responsibility without being able to do otherwise. So determinism is not a threat even if it rules out alternatives. This can be paired with:

Semi-compatibilism: Determinism may rule out alternatives (i.e. the freedom to do otherwise). But freedom to do otherwise is not the kind of freedom required for moral responsibility. Frankfurt-style counterexamples to the Principle of Alternative Possibilities show that the kind of freedom required for responsibility does not require alternatives (the Principle of Alternative Possibilities is false).

This is quite a complicated picture. It seems to leave us with no clear victor in the debate between compatibilism and incompatibilism. But thinking about alternative possibilities is not just a digression. It gets us thinking about what is required for responsibility. And it gets us thinking about why determinism either does or does not worry us when we are thinking about freedom and responsibility.

FURTHER READING

Aristotle provides some important foundational elements concerning the conditions of moral responsibility. For the relevant passages, see Aristotle, Book III of *The Nicomachean Ethics*, trans. Terence Irwin (Indianapolis, IN: Hackett Publishing Co., 1985).

For a helpful overview of the issue of moral responsibility, see Andrew Eshleman, "Moral Responsibility", in Edward N. Zalta (ed.), *The Stanford Encyclopedia of Philosophy* (Winter 2009 Edition), www.plato.stanford.edu/archives/win2009/entries/moral-responsibility.

For a classic statement and defense of the "shallow" notion of moral responsibility, see J.J.C. Smart, "Free Will, Praise, and Blame", *Mind*, 70 (1963): 291–306.

For P.F. Strawson's famous and influential discussion of reactive attitudes, see P.F. Strawson, "Freedom and Resentment", *Proceedings of the British Academy*, 48 (1962): 187–211. For discussion of Strawson's work, see Michael McKenna and Paul Russell (eds), *Free Will and Reactive Attitudes: Perspectives on P.F. Strawson's "Freedom and Resentment"* (Burlington, VT: Ashgate Publishing, 2008).

The following are all excellent collections of articles on moral responsibility: John Martin Fischer (ed.), *Moral Responsibility* (Ithaca, NY: Cornell University Press, 1986); John Martin Fischer and Mark Ravizza (eds), *Perspectives on Moral Responsibility* (Ithaca, NY: Cornell University Press, 1993); and Ferdinand Schoeman (ed.), *Responsibility, Character, and the Emotions* (New York: Cambridge University Press, 1987).

For seventeenth- and eighteenth-century classical compatibilism, see Thomas Hobbes, *Leviathan*, R.E. Flatman and D. Johnston (eds) (New York: W.W. Norton & Co, 1997); David Hume, *An Enquiry Concerning Human Understanding*, P.H. Nidditch (ed.) (Oxford: Clarendon Press, 1978); and David Hume, *A Treatise of Human Nature*, P.H. Nidditch (ed.) (Oxford: Clarendon Press, 1978).

For a twentieth-century defense of classical compatibilism, see A.J. Ayer, "Freedom and Necessity", in his *Philosophical Essays* (New York: St. Martin's Press, 1954), 3–20.

For some more current discussions of compatibilism, see Bernard Berofsky, "Ifs, Cans, and Free Will: The Issues", in Robert Kane (ed.), *The Oxford Handbook of Free Will*, (Oxford: Oxford University Press, 2002), 181-201; Ishtiyaque Haji, "Compatibilist Views of Freedom and Responsibility", in Robert Kane (ed.), *The Oxford Handbook of Free Will*, (Oxford: Oxford University Press, 2002); and Michael McKenna, "Compatibilism", in Edward N. Zalta (ed.), *The Stanford Encyclopedia of Philosophy* (Winter 2009 Edition), www.plato.stanford.edu/archives/win2009/entries/compatibilism.

For a more recent compatibilist analysis of "could have done otherwise", see Kadri Vihvelin, "Free Will Demystified: A Dispositional Account", *Philosophical Topics*, 32 (2004): 427–50.

There is an enormous literature on the Frankfurt-style counter-examples to the Principle of Alternative Possibilities. For Frankfurt's original paper, see Harry Frankfurt, "Alternate Possibilities and Moral Responsibility", *Journal of Philosophy*, 66 (1969): 829–39. For some of the more important further discussion of the cases, see John Martin Fischer, "Frankfurt-type Examples and Semi-Compatibilism", in Robert Kane (ed.), *The Oxford Handbook of Free Will*, (Oxford: Oxford University Press, 2002), 281-308; Carl Ginet, "In Defense of the Principle of Alternative Possibilities: Why I Don't Find Frankfurt's Argument Convincing", *Philosophical Perspectives*, 10 (1996): 403–17; Alfred Mele and David Robb, "Rescuing Frankfurt-Style Cases", *Philosophical Review*, 107 (1998): 97–112; and David Widerker, "Libertarianism and Frankfurt's Attack on the Principle of Alternative Possibilities", *Philosophical Review*, 104 (1995): 247–61.

SOME CURRENT COMPATIBILIST PROPOSALS

As we've already seen, compatibilists believe that free will is not threatened by **determinism**. According to **compatibilism**, even if determinism is true, we can still have the kind of free will required for **moral responsibility**. But how does the compatibilist make intuitive sense out of the idea that we can be free, even while everything we do, think, and feel is determined?

In the last chapter, we noted that **classical compatibilism** does this, in part, by characterizing free will as an unhindered ability to do what one wants. Determinism does not threaten this ability. Even if determinism is true, we can still often do what we want (it's just that we are determined to want what we want, and then to act on this want). But some might argue that this is not good enough because it leaves too many things open. It seems possible that someone could do what he wants without anyone getting in the way, but still not be free. Suppose that Dan suffers from delusions. He thinks, falsely, that some secret government agency is after him. Dan might gear his behavior towards trying to escape from his supposed pursuers. Dan could conceivably act on various desires that he has and do so unhindered by anyone or anything else. For example, he might wish to create a disguise for himself. Suppose that nothing hinders him from buying and using hair color, glasses, and a fake mustache. But it would be difficult to think that Dan is acting freely. His delusions have too much of a hold on him. This means that it's not enough to say that free will is doing what one wants unhindered.

MESH THEORIES

Nowadays, compatibilists seek to fill in some of the gaps left open by classical compatibilism. While classical compatibilist views focus on external impediments to action, more recent theories focus on internal obstacles and how these relate to choice and action. Some such theories are referred to as **mesh theories** because they claim that freedom consists in an appropriate mesh between various elements of an action and the agent's inner states. The basic idea behind such theories is that free will is centrally about how our choices and actions relate to our inner states. Are we able to choose and act on our own desires and reasons? Are we able to be whom and what we want to be? If so, it seems that we have the kind of freedom we care about and the kind that is required for moral responsibility. And if we can be whom and what we want to be, perhaps it does not matter whether determinism is true. These theories present a more complex picture of the relationship between various mental elements and our actions and of what has to be true in order to say that we are free.

A HIERARCHICAL MESH THEORY

Have you ever stepped back and taken a good look at your own desires? Have you ever thought about something you want and whether it is a good or a bad thing that you want it? Suppose you want Beluga caviar on a fairly regular basis. Perhaps when you reflect upon this desire, you find that this is something that you like about yourself. You are glad that you have such refined tastes and desire such things. Or alternatively, perhaps you wish you did not have this desire. This caviar is expensive and you wish you did not like it so much. If only you didn't get such cravings for it, you would be much happier. But since you crave it, you are either left with an unsatisfied craving or an empty bank account. Notice that in either scenario, you are engaging in self-evaluation. It seems pretty plausible to suggest that ordinary persons evaluate themselves in this way from time to time. Some mesh theories of free will and responsibility suggest that there's an important inner hierarchy involved in free will, one that involves just this sort of reflection upon one's own desires. One of the most famous and influential comes from Harry Frankfurt.

Frankfurt suggests that what is *distinctive* about us as persons is the ability to step back and reflect upon our own desires. Many kinds of non-persons have desires, or at least we have good reason to think they do. But these creatures do not evaluate their desires. For instance, my dog, as much as he might seem like a person to me, probably does not reflect upon his own desires. He certainly has desires. He wants to go to the dog park or for a walk. He wants to eat the cheese off the table. He wants to please his "parents". He might even have conflicting desires: "I want to listen to my mom who is telling me to stay". "I want to chase the squirrel". But it's doubtful that he ever reflects on these desires. He does not, for example, say, "I wish I did not want to chase the squirrel" or "I wish I did not want to be a good dog". His desires just are what they are and he does not evaluate them. Now, for all we know, this could be false. If my dog does evaluate his desires, then perhaps he is a person after all. But that is beside the point. The point here is to recognize that being able to evaluate desires is a special kind of ability that goes beyond just having desires. And Frankfurt claims that this ability to evaluate is something that enables us to have free will.

Frankfurt calls the products of these self-evaluations, **second-order desires**. Persons can "want to want". The difference between **first-order desires** and second-order desires has to do with the object of these desires. In other words, first-order desires and second-order desires pertain to different kinds of things. You might think of the object of a desire as an answer to the question, "what do I want?" With first-order desires the answer to this question will be some other kind of entity – a thing, state, or action (I want … caviar; … ice cream; … to be asleep; … to go to the mall; … to chase the squirrel). Second-order desires, unlike first-order desires, are desires that pertain to other desires. So the answer to "what do I want?" will be another desire. What do I want? To want. Or to not want. (I want to want caviar. I do not want to want caviar.) And these second-order desires seem unique to persons. So, whereas my dog does not think about whether he wants to want to chase the squirrel, we do this sort of thing on a somewhat regular basis. The smoker who is trying to quit may say, "I wish I did not want to smoke". The smoker is evaluating a first-order desire, to smoke, and saying that he does not want to have it. This second wish is a second-order desire.

We might say that the smoker who wishes he did not want to smoke is, in a sense, alienated from his own first-order desire to smoke. He does not identify with it. Although he wants to smoke, he does not want to want to smoke, so he feels like the desire that makes him smoke is not really his *own*. His first-order desire to smoke is, in a way, operating in spite of him. He might say, "I don't want to smoke, but this urge is making me". Suppose, on the other hand, that the smoker did want to want to smoke. In other words, suppose the smoker thinks about his desire for the cigarette and is perfectly content with it. Well, in that case, he does identify with his desire to smoke. He *owns* it, in a sense, and does not feel alienated from it. It's not operating against him.

FRANKFURT'S CHARACTERIZATION OF FREE WILL

Frankfurt characterizes the "will" as a certain kind of desire. We have a number of desires at any given time, but not all of them result in action. Right now, as I type, I have a desire to keep writing, as well as a mild desire for some coffee, and a longstanding desire to visit my relatives who live far away. But right now, these latter desires do not move me to act. I do not act on my desire for coffee. Too much caffeine will keep me awake all night. Nor do I act on my desire to visit relatives. To say the least, it would be impractical to jump into my car to drive ten hours every time I thought of my desire to see my relatives. But my desire to finish this chapter does lead me to act. The will, according to Frankfurt, is a desire that is *effective* – that is, it moves a person to act. So my "will" right now consists in my desire to finish the chapter.

Frankfurt calls desires about one's will, **second-order volitions**. On a view like this, *free will consists in having the will one wants*. Intuitively, the idea is that if we do what we want and the want is something we identify with and take ownership of, then how can we claim that we are not free? If I do what I want and my desire to do that thing is one that I want to have, then it seems to Frankfurt that I should be able to be held responsible. Suppose I want to punch you and I am perfectly happy with the fact that I want to punch you. Suppose I do punch you because of this desire. It then seems plausible to suggest that I should be blamed for this behavior. I did not do anything against my own will, regardless of what else is true. Just as the classical compatibilist will say that I am free if I am able to do what I want, Frankfurt adds that I have free will if I have the will that I want.

HOW IS THIS SUPPOSED TO SOLVE THE PROBLEM?

According to many philosophers, a successful characterization of free will should accord with our intuitions about when we are free and when we are not. The view should allow us to distinguish – in ways that make sense to us – cases in which we are free from cases in which we are not. The compatibilist claims that the most important differences between free and unfree actions have nothing to do with determinism. Thus, to be successful, a compatibilist needs to make a very strong case that his view really does show accurate distinctions between free and unfree that have nothing to do with determinism.

Frankfurt's view is a compatibilist view because the way it characterizes free will is consistent with determinism. Because free will is understood as a relationship among one's own desires, as long as this relationship is right, it doesn't matter whether it was determined. Even if determinism is true, I can still have the will that I want, it's just that I will be determined to have that will and to want it. But for Frankfurt, that is not a problem, since what really matters is whether I have the proper internal mesh. Am I alienated from the forces that are motivating me to act, or aren't I? And Frankfurt's view distinguishes between free and unfree in ways that have nothing to do with determinism. The difference between someone who identifies with her will and someone who does not is not about determinism. Determinism has nothing to do with it. According to Frankfurt, we get intuitively plausible results with this view. Those who are alienated from their own motivations do not seem free to us.

Frankfurt's view has been extremely influential and important. Although some philosophers have raised difficult challenges to the view, many of these same philosophers have built upon Frankfurt's ideas in their own theories.

OBJECTIONS

Despite its appeal, there are some drawbacks to Frankfurt's theory. The view has the following results. Suppose that Kevin is a kleptomaniac – he has an irresistible desire to steal things. Suppose that Kevin hates the fact that he has this desire and wishes that he did not have it. On Frankfurt's view, we would say that Kevin's will is not free. Suppose that Katy is also a kleptomaniac. But suppose that Katy likes being a kleptomaniac. She is glad she has the desire to steal. Frankfurt's view suggests that Katy's case is importantly different. Katy is not alienated from her own will. She does not have the sense that her will is operating without her blessing. She owns it and identifies with it. Therefore, according to Frankfurt, Katy is blameworthy. On the one hand, this makes sense because someone who is content with always stealing things does seem worthy of moral disdain. But others might think that it is counterintuitive to think of Kevin and Katy differently in terms of their moral agency, since they have the same compulsion.

Another problem has to do with what philosophers call an "infinite regress". In this case, the worry is that there could be a regress of volitions (third-order, fourth-order, and so on). Frankfurt's original worry is that we could be alienated from our will and therefore not have free will. But why couldn't we be alienated from a second-order volition? In other words, couldn't I want to want to eat cake, but be alienated from this second-order want? In order for the second-order want to be free, don't I need to evaluate it on a higher level and want it from this level? But then where does this chain stop? Hence, the infinite regress.

Finally, some philosophers bring up manipulation. According to Frankfurt's theory, a person has free will so long as the action comes from the will the person wants to have. But imagine a case in which the person was brainwashed into wanting to want. Frankfurt's theory says that all that matters is the internal mesh. But doesn't it seem like we ought to care about where our wants came from? If I have been manipulated into having the desires that I have, am I really free? Frankfurt's theory would seem to have the result that I am. Perhaps

Frankfurt could insist that those who have been manipulated are exceptions and should not be counted as free. But then it will be difficult for him to justify why determinism does not interfere with freedom. In other words, it is hard to see, on his view, how manipulation would be importantly different from determinism.

Frankfurt has responded to some of these worries, and others have responded to him yet again. But I will leave the debate to the interested reader.

THE REASON VIEW

Philosopher Susan Wolf calls Frankfurt's view, and others like it, **real self (or deep self) views**, because they base freedom and responsibility on whether the will or the action comes from something the agent identifies with as part of his real desires. In other words, on such views, an agent acts with free will when what he does expresses his "real self". But Wolf does not subscribe to a real self view. Instead, she advocates a different kind of mesh theory. She calls her theory the **Reason View**.

You may have noticed that Frankfurt's view keeps everything about freedom and responsibility wrapped up within the agent. As long as everything inside is fitting together appropriately, the agent is free and responsible. It doesn't matter so much what's going on outside of me, as long as I have the will that I want. If I want to have the desire to eat cake, then it doesn't seem to matter where this desire came from, or whether I am capable of recognizing the drawbacks of, say, eating cake for breakfast. Wolf, while she likes the idea of a mesh between an agent's actions and values, thinks the agent must also be properly connected to the world outside of herself.

She calls her view the Reason View because she thinks it is crucial that the agent be able to understand and value the best reasons for acting. The agent must have access to what Wolf calls the True and the Good. We need to be able to do the right thing for the right reasons in order to be held responsible. Someone who does not have access to these things is not responsible in the same way. For instance, there could be cases in which a person had a horribly deprived childhood and was not able to learn right and wrong. Such a person might be incapable of recognizing the True and the Good and thus cannot be held responsible. So it is not just whether the action and will accord with an agent's real self. The agent must also be able to recognize the world for the way it is. To be responsible, someone must be able to see what is good and see this as a reason for acting.

ASYMMETRY OF PRAISE AND BLAME

In American folklore there is a story about George Washington when he was a young boy. According to the story, George had a hatchet that he loved to use. In his enthusiasm for using his hatchet, he chopped down his father's favorite cherry tree. When his father confronted him, little George purportedly said, "I cannot tell a lie" and then confessed what he had done. His father was proud of him for telling the truth. How do we feel about George Washington when he allegedly said, "I cannot tell a lie"? Do we find this praiseworthy? If we take George at his word, George cannot help but tell the truth. Does that mean he does not have the kind of freedom required for moral responsibility? Wolf thinks that George would clearly be praiseworthy, even if he literally could not do anything but tell the truth. Wolf's view has a very interesting asymmetry. In the last chapter, we talked about the relevance of being able to do otherwise. Wolf contends that the ability to do otherwise does matter, but only with respect to wrong actions and blameworthiness. She thinks that if someone is going to be blamed for something, it is only fair that he could have done otherwise. So if George had lied, but had been unable to avoid lying, we cannot blame him. But with respect to right actions and praiseworthiness, Wolf claims that it is not necessary to be able to do otherwise. If a person did the right thing for the right reasons (i.e. was able to recognize the True and the Good), then an ability to do otherwise is irrelevant. Hence the old story about George Washington. Supposing that he literally could not have lied, this is presumably due to his character, upbringing, and so on. According to Wolf, this should not detract from his praiseworthiness. Just because George could not have done otherwise, we do not say, "not responsible". We still praise him. In fact, we might praise him all the more because his character is that strong. Notice that this asymmetry arises because Wolf's view centers on an agent's ability to connect to the True and the Good. If an agent does the right thing for the right reasons, then he is able to appreciate and recognize the True and the Good, so it does not matter whether there is an ability to do otherwise.

HOW IS THIS SUPPOSED TO SOLVE THE PROBLEM?

The Reason View is a compatibilist view. But the asymmetry makes this a little more complicated. Since Wolf thinks that the ability to do otherwise is required for blameworthiness, this means that she thinks being able to do otherwise is compatible with determinism. We saw earlier that it is difficult to come up with such an account (we saw why the **Conditional Analysis** did not work so well). But Wolf does not need to worry about the ability to do otherwise when it comes to praiseworthiness (and some philosophers think she should give up the asymmetry and say that the ability to do otherwise is never required, for reasons discussed in Chapter 3). It's easier to see with praiseworthy actions why determinism would not threaten them according to her account. Someone who does the right thing for the right reasons is praiseworthy regardless of whether determined to do so. If George Washington really cannot tell a lie, we still think he is praiseworthy for telling the truth. So even if determinism means that we can never do otherwise, it doesn't matter as long as we are able to do the right thing for the right reasons.

OBJECTIONS

A major objection to Wolf's view is similar to an objection to Frankfurt's view. Some philosophers claim that Wolf's view is subject to the same kind of manipulation worry. Couldn't an agent be brainwashed or manipulated into accessing the True and the Good? Suppose an agent was hypnotized or otherwise brainwashed into doing the right thing for the right reasons. Suppose George had been brainwashed into always telling the truth. We tend to think that manipulation and brainwashing rules out freedom. And once again, if Wolf says that manipulation rules out free will, then it is going to be hard for her to show why determinism does not. There are, of course, ways of responding here. Perhaps it is not possible to brainwash someone into doing something *for the right reasons*. But again, I will leave the debate to the interested reader to pursue.

REASONS-RESPONSIVENESS AND GUIDANCE CONTROL

REASONS-RESPONSIVENESS

The last kind of compatibilist view we will look at characterizes free will in terms of the ability to respond to reasons. The basic intuition here is that we are free in the sense required for moral responsibility when we are able to act according to reasons and when we are sensitive to reasons in the right way. This does not mean that we are only free if we are in fact acting rationally or doing what we have most reason to do. It just means that we must be *capable*, in a certain sense, of responding appropriately to reasons, whether we in fact do appropriately respond to them. We are not free if reasons are ineffective – that is, when we are *not able* to respond to them.

How can we tell whether someone is able to respond to reasons? Suppose Rory is deciding whether to practice the piano. Rory has a piano lesson tomorrow and is not quite prepared for it. He decides to practice. Is Rory reasons-responsive in this scenario? Although Rory's action seems to be guided by reasons, it's difficult to say whether he is reasons-responsive without knowing more. Just because there are good reasons for Rory to practice does not mean that he is reasons-responsive. It could be, for example, that Rory is just a compulsive practicer and cannot help himself. But how can we tell if someone is in fact reasons-responsive? Being able to tell in the real world poses certain challenges. We may just have to make our best guess based on what we know about Rory and about human psychology.

But even if knowing in the real world has its practical obstacles, philosophers think it's important to determine a theoretical basis for being able to distinguish between **reasons-responsiveness** and non-responsiveness. In other words, philosophers want to determine *what we would need to know* in order to be able to tell whether there is reasons-responsiveness in a given case. Some philosophers have suggested that reasons-responsiveness can be determined by looking at whether the action would have been different had other reasons (favoring a different action) presented themselves. We can't know this for certain in the real world, because we can't rewind and see what would have happened had there been different reasons at work.

For example, we can't "rewind" and change the circumstances to know what Rory would in fact do under these altered circumstances. But we can theorize about this. If we can hypothetically give Rory some different reasons and determine whether he would respond differently, we can know whether he is capable of responding to reasons or whether he is insensitive to them. For example, suppose we hypothetically add the circumstance that Rory's lesson has been cancelled this week. Furthermore, Rory just found out he has a math exam in two days. Would Rory still practice the piano, or might he decide to study for his exam? If the latter, then there is reasons-responsiveness. But perhaps in light of this different information, Rory would still practice anyway. Does this mean there is no reasons-responsiveness? Not necessarily. It could just be that the exam and the rescheduling are not strong enough reasons. Maybe there are other reasons that would lead to a different action by Rory. Philosophers have a lot to say about just what level of responsiveness is required. But in any case, we can say that if Rory would practice the piano *no matter what* (no matter what kinds of reasons presented themselves) then it seems that he is not really capable of responding to reasons.

It might seem odd to use this sort of hypothetical reasoning. But it's not really so strange to use this kind of reasoning to understand a capacity like responsiveness. To further illuminate the idea, here's an analogy that focuses on a different kind of responsiveness. Think of a heating and cooling system in a house. The system has a thermostat that detects the temperature. If the temperature is too low, the heating system kicks on to heat the house. The heating system "responds" to the temperature. Suppose the heat kicks on one day at 12:05pm. We might at first assume that this means that the system is responsive to temperature. But this assumption may be mistaken. What if the heating system is not responding to the temperature but is instead just set to turn on at 12:05pm? Or perhaps the system is malfunctioning and the heat just turns on at 12:05pm regardless of what else is true. To decide whether the system is responsive to temperature, we must determine whether the system would have responded differently had the temperature been relevantly different. We think about this hypothetically: would it have responded differently? Now, with a heating system, we can also perhaps test this in a real-world way. But even if we do, we are still utilizing hypothetical reasoning: what would it do under different circumstances? Likewise, reasons–responsiveness looks at what would happen given different circumstances.

The reasons–responsiveness view is meant to capture our intuitions about certain cases. For example, suppose someone has a genuine psychological compulsion or phobia. Such a person might act on that compulsion or phobia without being responsive to reasons. In other words, even if the person had had very good reasons not to engage in the behavior, she would have engaged in it anyway. For example, suppose I am horribly afraid of spiders. Suppose that I am in my colleague's office when I notice that he has brought his pet tarantula to work with him today. I quickly leave the room. Was my leaving a "free" action? Was I reasons–responsive on this occasion? How can we tell? In the "real world" it will be difficult. But theoretically we might ask the following kinds of questions: would I have left the room even if I had had good reasons not to? Would I have backed away from the spider no matter what? Suppose I needed some extra cash and my colleague offered me 1,000 dollars to stay in the room with the spider. Would I have stayed? If my phobia is strong enough, perhaps no reasons would be sufficient to make me stay. Thus, my phobia is enough to take away my free will and responsibility.

GUIDANCE CONTROL

The most important, well-developed and influential reasons–responsiveness view is espoused by John Fischer and Mark Ravizza. They argue that reasons–responsiveness is the key to free will. They also argue for something they call **guidance control**. On their view, guidance control requires a moderate level of reasons–responsiveness. (They distinguish between weak, moderate, and strong reasons–responsiveness. I will set these details aside.)

Guidance control starts out with the intuition that when we act freely, we have control over our actions. A person with free will is someone who guides his own behavior. If I didn't guide my behavior, how could I be responsible for it? But Fischer and Ravizza point out that there are different kinds of control. They dub one kind of control **regulative control**. Regulative control involves alternative possibilities – being able to do otherwise. They use the analogy of steering a car. Regulative control means being able to steer the car to the right or to the left. The debate over the **Principle of Alternative Possibilities** (in the last chapter) is a debate over whether regulative control is required for freedom and responsibility.

Fischer and Ravizza do not think regulative control is necessary for free will. They are convinced by the **Frankfurt-style counter-examples** to the Principle of Alternative Possibilities. But control of some kind is required. They claim that what we need is guidance control. To go back to the car analogy, guidance control would be like being able to steer the car but only to the left. One is still guiding the car, but there is no ability to do otherwise. The intuition here is that what matters for freedom and responsibility is the "actual sequence" of the action. In other words, what matters is that I actually guided my action. It is irrelevant whether I could have done something else. As we have seen, "could have" pertains to something that did not in fact happen. According to the guidance control view, what matters is what did in fact happen. If I was the one steering the car to the left, then it does not matter whether I could have steered it to the right.

MECHANISMS

But how does guidance control fit together with reasons-responsiveness? How do the two parts of their view fit together? Recall that on this view, it is crucial to be able to respond to reasons. But reasons-responsiveness depends on whether one could have responded to different reasons and done something else, had these reasons presented themselves. But here's the problem. Doesn't this sound like the view is requiring regulative control, that is, an ability to do otherwise? Fischer and Ravizza do not think regulative control is required. So how do these two elements (reasons-responsiveness and guidance control) fit together?

Here Fischer and Ravizza make a distinction between different kinds of views. They say that some views are agent-based and some are based on what they call the **mechanism** the agent uses in acting. Their view is mechanism-based. A mechanism is just whatever process issues in the action – basically, whatever way the action is caused. So, in many normal cases, we can say that an agent acted from a "practical reasoning" mechanism. In contrast, direct brain stimulation by the evil neurosurgeon would be a different kind of mechanism. So would a compulsive desire.

On their view, the agent does not need to be able to do otherwise, but the mechanism used in the action needs to be responsive to reasons. So, having a mechanism that is responsive to reasons does not amount to the *agent* being able to do otherwise. For example, recall one of the Frankfurt-style counterexamples to the Principle of Alternative Possibilities (Chapter 3). In one of these examples, Kathy wants to kill Virginia and does so, on her own. Meanwhile, Ned has been waiting in the wings, ready to intervene if he has to in order to make Kathy kill Virginia if she does not do so on her own. But Kathy does so on her own, so Ned just sits back and watches. Kathy, in this scenario, could not have done otherwise. She was going to kill Virginia regardless (because Ned would have made her). But her mechanism − the process that resulted in her killing Virginia − could very well have been responsive to reasons. In other words, presumably, Kathy killed Virginia based on "normal" practical reasoning. This kind of mechanism is reasons–responsive. Kathy could not have avoided killing Virginia, but her practical reasoning mechanism could have been responsive.

It might seem puzzling to think that the mechanism is responsive when she is not. But it's not as counterintuitive as it may sound. Fischer and Ravizza are not suggesting that the mechanism could do things without Kathy. Instead, they are just assessing whether the mechanism is appropriately sensitive. The way to tell if a mechanism is sensitive is to think of hypothetical scenarios and see if it would respond otherwise. These hypothetical scenarios are not possibilities that are really open to Kathy (they are not accessible to her). But they are relevant in telling us about the sensitivity of the mechanism.

Think back to the analogy to the heating and cooling system in a house. Imagine that the residents want the house to be 72 degrees. At 10am, the system detects that the temperature is rising above 72. It then turns on the air, so that the house will cool. As we said before, the system has a mechanism that is responsive to temperatures. This means that *had the temperature been much lower at 10am*, the mechanism would have responded differently. But − and this is the key point − the fact that the mechanism is responsive does not mean that the system was able to do otherwise than it in fact did at 10am. At 10am, the temperature was in fact just above 72, so the cooling system does not have access to the scenario in which the temperature is much lower. The system cannot control the weather! The lower temperature scenario is a hypothetical situation that allows us to determine whether the mechanism is a responsive kind of mechanism. Likewise, just because an agent acts from a reasons-responsive mechanism, this does not mean that she could have in fact done otherwise at the time. (This is just an analogy of course, designed to show why Fischer and Ravizza use a mechanism based approach. One should note that on their view, we are not like machines! Our ability to evaluate and respond to reasons is unique and gives us the power to express ourselves in ways that make us responsible for our behavior. Machines are presumably not responsible for theirs.)

HOW IS THIS SUPPOSED TO SOLVE THE PROBLEM?

Fischer and Ravizza's view is a very sophisticated and compelling compatibilist view. It is supposed to solve the problem by showing that what we really care about when it comes to free will and responsibility is guidance control, spelled out in terms of reasons-responsiveness. And both of these things are consistent with determinism. I can still guide my behavior if determinism is true. Determinism does not do it for me. And the mechanisms I use when I act can be responsive to reasons if determinism is true. Even if it was determined that I would have the reasons that I have and respond to the reasons to which I respond, the mechanism I use in acting can be responsive to reasons. This is like saying that the thermostat could be responsive to temperatures, whether or not determinism is true. In other words, even if it was determined that it be 72 degrees at 10am and that the thermostat detect this and the system respond appropriately, none of that negates the fact that the thermostat is responsive. What we want from free will is to be able to guide our behavior according to our reasons. If we act from mechanisms which are responsive, then this is exactly what we are doing. We are unfree when we act from a mechanism which is not appropriately responsive – that is, when the same behavior would result regardless of the reasons.

OBJECTIONS

Because this view is so sophisticated and complex, there are some objections that we will not be able to discuss here. But I will mention one important objection. This one should sound kind of familiar. This is an objection based on manipulation. Suppose an evil neurosurgeon messes with someone's brain and implants a reasons-responsive mechanism. This would not seem like a case in which we should hold an agent morally responsible, even though the reasons-responsiveness view would suggest that we should.

In order to respond to this worry, Fischer and Ravizza add something to their theory. They suggest that the agent must take responsibility for the mechanisms that are used in acting. In other words, they suggest that the agent is only responsible if the agent is acting from a reasons-responsive mechanism that is "owned" by the agent. The agent does this through a process of moral development. Ownership involves coming to see that one is the source of one's behavior (when acting from the mechanism in question) and that this behavior has real effects in the world. An agent will not be responsible for a mechanism inserted by an evil neurosurgeon then, because the agent will not have had a chance to take responsibility for it throughout growth and moral development.

But this is not the end of the story. Manipulation cases can be constructed that include the agent's "taking responsibility" for the mechanism. So Fischer and Ravizza will need to say what to do with such cases. Fischer has responded to such cases but I will leave his responses to the interested reader to pursue.

SUMMARY

In this chapter, we looked at three different kinds of current compatibilist proposals. First, we discussed a hierarchical mesh theory made famous by Harry Frankfurt. On this kind of view, free will is about whether one's internal states are in order. Am I alienated from my own motivations or does my will line up with how I want to be? Do I feel as if my desires are in charge and acting without my participation, or do I identify with them and feel like I am acting from my deeper self – from who I really am? Such a view is compatible with determinism, because determinism is irrelevant to whether my inner states and actions are properly meshed. If they are, I am free, regardless of whether these inner states have all been determined by prior causes.

The second view we looked at is Susan Wolf's Reason View. On such a view, we are free if we are able to act according to the True and the Good. If I am able to do the right thing for the right reasons, it does not matter whether I have been determined to do so. If George Washington was unable to lie because he was determined to tell the truth, it does not matter. He is still praiseworthy. But if things had been different and George was unable to access the right reasons – perhaps due to a very deprived childhood, then he could not be blamed for doing something wrong.

Finally, we looked at a complex reasons-responsiveness view. This kind of view is similar to Wolf's view in that it requires the appropriate connection to reasons. But it is based on the idea that what matters is whether there is an appropriate sensitivity to reasons. If I have a compulsion or neurotic disorder whereby reasons just have no influence, then I am not responsible for what I do. But if reasons play the proper role, then I can be held responsible. This view is compatible with determinism because there can still be sensitivity to reasons even if determinism is true. Suppose I eat a piece of cake. It does not matter whether I was determined to eat the cake. What matters is how I was determined. If I ate it out of a compulsion that is completely insensitive to reasons (cake would be eaten regardless of what reasons presented themselves), then I can't be held responsible. But if I ate it from a kind of practical reasoning mechanism that does respond to reasons, then I can be held responsible.

FURTHER READING

For some good general resources on different kinds of compatibilist views, see Ishtiyaque Haji, "Compatibilist Views of Freedom and Responsibility", in Robert Kane (ed.), *The Oxford Handbook of Free Will* (Oxford and New York: Oxford University Press, 2002), 202–28. Both this edition and the 2nd edition (2011) have some other helpful articles on compatibilism. See also Michael McKenna, "Compatibilism", in Edward N. Zalta (ed.), *The Stanford Encyclopedia of Philosophy* (Winter 2009 Edition), www.plato. stanford.edu/archives/win2009/entries/compatibilism/; and Ferdinand Schoeman (ed.), *Responsibility, Character, and the Emotions: New Essays in Moral Psychology* (Cambridge: Cambridge University Press, 1987).

For Harry Frankfurt's hierarchical mesh theory, see Harry Frankfurt, "Freedom of the Will and the Concept of a Person", *Journal of Philosophy*, 68 (1971): 5–20; and Harry Frankfurt, "Identification and Wholeheartedness", in Schoeman (ed.), 27–45. For scholarly discussion of his view, see Sarah Buss and Lee Overton (eds), *Contours of Agency: Essays on Themes from Harry Frankfurt* (Cambridge, MA: MIT Press, 2002).

For Susan Wolf's Reason View, see Susan Wolf, "Sanity and the Metaphysics of Responsibility", in Schoeman (ed.), 45–64; and Susan Wolf, *Freedom within Reason* (Oxford: Oxford University Press, 1990).

For Fischer and Ravizza's guidance control view, see John Martin Fischer and Mark Ravizza, *Responsibility and Control: An Essay on Moral Responsibility* (Cambridge: Cambridge University Press, 1998). For further discussion of this view, see John Martin Fischer, *My Way: Essays on Moral Responsibility*, (New York: Oxford University Press, 2006); John Martin Fischer, *Deep Control: Essays on Free Will and Value* (New York: Oxford University Press, 2011); and John Martin Fischer, Robert Kane, Derk Pereboom, and Manuel Vargas, *Four Views on Free Will* (Malden, MA: Blackwell Publishers, 2007).

5

SOME CURRENT INCOMPATIBILIST PROPOSALS

For those who remain unconvinced that **moral responsibility** and freedom are compatible with **determinism**, this chapter will provide a number of alternatives. Recall that **incompatibilism** is the view that free will and determinism cannot exist together. Thus, some incompatibilist theories claim that because determinism appears to be false, there is room for free will. **Libertarianism** is a kind of incompatibilism according to which we sometimes have free will. There are three basic varieties of libertarianism (with considerable variation within each category): **simple indeterminism**, **event-causal libertarianism**, and **agent causation (or agent-causal libertarianism)**.

But recall also that not all incompatibilists endorse free will. Some think that we do not have free will, either because they believe that determinism is true, or because they believe that both determinism and **indeterminism** are incompatible with free will. These views are called **hard determinism** and **hard incompatibilism**.

This chapter will discuss all of these general incompatibilist categories.

LIBERTARIAN VIEWS

SIMPLE INDETERMINISM

Do you ever feel as if you do something spontaneously and intentionally? It often seems to me as if I do. For example, I spontaneously raise my hand, turn on the computer, smile at a friend, or make a decision to go to the movies. It's not that these actions are without rhyme or reason. But they feel as if I am making them happen without anything making me bring them about. And perhaps nothing *is* making me perform them. Perhaps our free and intentional actions are, at their roots, *uncaused*. Simple indeterminism is the view that when we act freely there is an uncaused **basic mental action**. A basic mental action is just what the name implies. It is basic, meaning that it is not a complex process composed of other actions. And it is mental, meaning that it is to be distinguished from a bodily movement or what philosophers sometimes call an "overt" action. Examples of basic mental actions are choices, decisions, volitions (i.e. willings), and tryings. Sometimes a basic mental action just is the entire action. In other words, sometimes we just act by doing something in or with our minds, rather than by making any bodily movements. So, I make a decision without moving my body and this is my action. Other times, the basic mental action is the beginning of a more complex action. So, perhaps I raise my hand and this action begins with a volition – I *will* to raise my hand. The volition then causes a chain of events culminating in my arm's rising. Simple indeterminism is the view that all free actions either are, or begin with, *uncaused* basic mental actions.

Carl Ginet espouses an interesting and important version of simple indeterminism. Ginet suggests that uncaused basic mental actions are characterized by an "actish phenomenal quality". A **phenomenal quality** is the way something seems or feels to us – i.e. how we experience it. So if something has an "actish phenomenal quality", it feels like an action. What Ginet means here is that the event feels to us as if we are *making it happen*. So when I make a decision, or will to raise my arm, it seems to me that I am making the decision or the willing occur. It does not, for example, feel as if someone is inserting the decision into my head or that it is just popping into my head. Notice that this experience of willing is different from the experience I would have if my arm were hooked up to some sort of machine that caused the muscles to contract, thereby making my arm go up. In that case, I would not feel as if I were causing a volition which then made my arm go up. There would be no "actish phenomenal quality". But although it feels to us as if we are making basic mental actions occur, on Ginet's view, these events must be wholly uncaused if they are going to be free. It is also part of Ginet's view that although these basic actions must be uncaused, the rest of a complex action can be caused by the basic mental action. For instance, if I freely raise my hand to ask a question, the volition to do so is uncaused, but this volition then causes my arm's going up.

HOW IS THIS SUPPOSED TO SOLVE THE PROBLEM?

Simple indeterminism is an incompatibilist libertarian view. It is supposed to solve the problem of free will by showing how it is that our actions can be both uncaused and up to us. Unlike the compatibilist views we discussed in the last chapter, this view need not explain how an action can be up to us even though necessitated by a prior cause. On this view, determinism is false and some of our actions are uncaused. On Ginet's view, for example, if we act with an intention and this action is uncaused (or the basic action at the beginning is uncaused), then why not think that the action is up to us? After all, who else would it be up to?

OBJECTIONS

There are four important objections to Ginet's view (the latter two of which may plague any simple indeterminist view). The first concern is that the "actish phenomenal quality" does not seem to be good enough to secure the activeness that is required for true agency. For example, this quality might be present even if activeness is not. Suppose a crazy neuroscientist is manipulating my brain and causing me to feel as if I am bringing about my volition. Ginet himself has admitted that this is possible on his view. But then this means that my basic mental "action" could have this quality and not really be an action at all, but just something that is happening in my brain.

The second worry is perhaps a more serious one, and a worry that will probably arise for any simple indeterminist view. This is a worry about control. Although it might be tempting to think of freedom as being opposed to control, the kind of freedom we seem to care about for moral responsibility and authorship involves being in control of our own actions. How could I be held responsible for something I have done if I had no control over doing it? According to opponents of this view, simple indeterminism has a harder time accounting for control because it postulates that our free actions are uncaused. It is difficult to explain control without appealing to causation. For example, if I control the path of a boat, it seems plausible to suppose that this is because I *cause* it to go the way that it does. Control seems like a causal notion. How can I control an action that is completely uncaused, even by me?

Ginet and other simple indeterminists respond that we should not confuse the control of other kinds of events with our control of our own actions. Some simple indeterminists say that actions are "intrinsically" controlled, meaning that it is just in virtue of its being my action that I control it, even though it is uncaused. Ginet suggests that if a decision, say, is uncaused, then the agent can make it the case that she decided, just by deciding. She controls the decision just by doing it. She need not cause herself to decide, or have something else cause her to. If my smiling at my friend is uncaused (that is, my volition to smile is uncaused), I control this smiling just by smiling. I need not have control over my control.

The third objection is somewhat related. This is often called **the problem of luck**. As has been mentioned in earlier chapters, philosophers worry that if an action is not determined, then it is a matter of chance or luck that *it* occurred rather than an alternative action that could have occurred instead. If nothing about me prior to my decision determines it, then isn't it just an accident or fluke that this decision occurs? Given all the same things about me – the things I'm thinking about right before I act, my character, my desires, and so on – the action might not have occurred. Suppose when someone asks me if I like his shirt (I do not), I decide to lie to spare his feelings. Right before my decision, I think about how I would feel if someone criticized me, I think about my desire to avoid hurting anyone's feelings, and so on. But according to simple indeterminism, none of these factors cause my decision. That means that given these same factors, I could just as easily have decided to tell the truth. Then how can I be responsible for what I do in these cases? Ginet suggests that this kind of worry is misplaced because it generalizes from considerations about regular events and applies it to actions. Actions, according to Ginet, are very different. (Note that on his view, those thoughts and desires can still function as reasons that explain my action, they just cannot function as causes. More is said about this below.) But this is an important and ongoing debate. It is one we will revisit several times.

The fourth objection has to do with explaining an action in terms of the agent's reasons. It is typically understood that when an agent acts with free will and performs an intentional action, this action can be explained in terms of her reasons for doing it. How do we explain my act of deciding to go to the store? Well, I see that we are out of bread and I would like to have some in the house. So I have a reason for deciding to go to the store (that I want to get bread and I believe that going to the store is the way to satisfy this desire). But often when we are explaining some occurrence, we cite its causes. How to explain a tornado? Well, we look at the weather patterns that caused it to happen. How to explain a car accident? Same thing. We look to the causal factors. What caused the accident to occur? According to many philosophers, then, the way to explain an action is also in terms of its causes. But intentional actions are actions done for reasons. Perhaps then, reasons are causes. On this view, my reasons for deciding to go to the store caused me to make this decision.

But the simple indeterminist cannot allow reasons to be causes. If all free and intentional actions are uncaused, then they obviously aren't caused by reasons (since they are not caused by anything!). But such actions are still presumably done for reasons, since they are meant to be intentional. They are not supposed to be inexplicable. And they should be explicable in terms of the agent's reasons. If I slap you intentionally and you ask me why, presumably I should be able to cite a reason for doing so, even if this reason is just "because I had an urge" or "because I felt like it". If I literally had no reason at all, it seems difficult to understand this as an intentional action. But such "**reason explanations**" cannot be causal according to the simple indeterminist. But what, then, are they?

In the philosophical study of human action there is a longstanding debate between causalists and non-causalists about reason explanations. Causalists say that reasons must be causes in order to explain the action. Non-causalists often say that reasons provide **teleological explanations**. Teleological explanations are explanations in terms of the goal or purpose of something. Thus, a teleological explanation of an action does not answer "what brought it about?" but instead answers "what was it for?" (or "at what purpose or goal was it directed?"). Here is an example of the difference between a teleological explanation and a causal explanation (some philosophers suggest that teleological explanations *are* causal, but we will not get into that debate here). Suppose we want an explanation for why there is a statue of Barack Obama in the town square. A teleological explanation might cite the purpose of the statue: it is there to honor Obama or to commemorate his Presidency or some such thing. This is the goal or purpose of the statue. A causal explanation, on the other hand, would explain the statue by talking about what brought it about. This explanation might cite the sculptor and the workers who installed the statue in the square.

Again, simple indeterminists must be non-causalists about reasons. So people like Ginet must claim that reasons need not cause actions in order to explain them. According to Ginet, the only requirements are that while the action is being performed the agent remembers the appropriate desire (to get bread) and has an intention that her action (going to the store) satisfy the desire. This, he suggests, should be enough to explain that I went to the store for the reason that I wanted to get bread. Causalists do not think this response is sufficient. But there are good arguments on both sides. It is an ongoing debate that I will leave to the interested reader to pursue.

EVENT-CAUSAL LIBERTARIANISM

For a long time, the debate between compatibilists and libertarians (incompatibilists who believe in free will) was really a debate between causalists and non-causalists. Philosophers used to talk about the plausibility of "contra-causal freedom". It was assumed that causes would necessitate their effects, thus the only two options for free will were to suppose that free willings or actions were deterministically caused or to suppose that they were uncaused (as the simple indeterminists still believe). But in the twentieth century, some philosophers started to think that perhaps not all causes were deterministic. In other words, perhaps something could cause an event without necessitating it. Perhaps a cause could influence or make something more likely without forcing it to happen. Advances in quantum physics were starting to make it look like the world was not deterministic after all. And it was starting to look as if some events, rather than necessitating subsequent events, merely gave the subsequent events a certain likelihood of occurring.

Some free will theorists thought these kinds of advances in the theories of physics and causation allowed for new possibilities for free will. Perhaps indeterministic or **probabilistic causation** could reconcile free will with our place in the natural world. Elizabeth Anscombe, one of the pioneers of the idea that causation need not amount to necessitation, suggested that **laws of nature** could be like the rules of chess. The rules of chess do not dictate exactly what the player does, but they do constrain what he does. Thus, in acting, we don't break laws of nature – we play by the rules – but these rules do not force us into specific moves (i.e. actions).

One of the most important free will theories to come out of this advance is Robert Kane's theory. To explain his view, let's look at one of his examples. He asks us to imagine that a businesswoman (I will call her Brenda) is late for an important meeting. As she frantically makes her way to her meeting, she sees an assault taking place in an alley. She is faced with the decision of whether to stop and call for help, or whether to continue on to her very important meeting. Brenda knows that the moral thing to do is to stop and call for help. But her career ambitions are also pulling at her. Kane suggests that sometimes when we are faced with important moral decisions like these, it is undetermined which choice we will make. He calls these undetermined choices **self-forming actions (SFAs)** because it is through important choices such as these that we form our own characters. By making a decision in such a case, we partly determine who we are and we influence future decisions. Kane claims that the internal conflict that we experience when trying to make such decisions corresponds to a physical – in this case neuro-logical – indeterminacy. Chaos is stirred up in our brains due to the inner conflict. So for Brenda, her job ambitions and her moral inclinations interact with one another to result in indeterminacy. It is undetermined whether Brenda will choose to stay or choose to go. But unlike the simple indeterminist, Kane's view holds that her eventual choice is caused. If she chooses to stay, this will be caused by her moral inclinations (her reasons for staying). If she chooses to go, this will be caused by her ambitiousness (her reasons for going).

An interesting element of Kane's view is that Brenda is trying to make both choices at the same time. When Brenda makes her decision, say, to stay, this means that the decision to stay has overcome the **indeterminism** that is coming from her effort to make the competing decision. This is why we can hold her responsible for what she does *either way*. If she resists her desire to go to the meeting, we can praise her for staying because she was making an effort to choose this option. If, on the other hand, she gives in to her desire, then we can blame her because she made this effort. Kane cites our brain's capability to engage in parallel processing in order to support his idea that we can make two efforts at once. If Brenda were only trying to make the decision to stay, then it would not make as much sense to blame her if she decided to go, since she was not trying to do this (perhaps we could say that she did not try hard enough to decide to stay, but this is not quite the same thing).

HOW IS THIS SUPPOSED TO SOLVE THE PROBLEM?

Kane's interesting and intricate view proposes to resolve some of the major problems with both compatibilism and simple indeterminism. Because self-forming actions are undetermined, we need not worry about how to reconcile freedom and responsibility with determinism. But because they are not wholly uncaused, Kane claims that we avoid the biggest worries faced by the simple indeterminist. If we think control is a causal notion, then event-causalists like Kane will say that the agent still controls her action even though it is not determined. This is because it is not uncaused. And unlike the simple indeterminist, the event-causalist can allow that reason explanations are causal explanations, thus avoiding some of the difficulties of holding that reasons explain without causing. On Kane's view, for example, either way that Brenda chooses, we can say that her reasons for that choice caused it. Again, Kane suggests that Brenda is responsible for her choice either way because she is making dual efforts of will. One effort is geared towards making the choice to stay, and one is geared towards making the choice to go.

OBJECTIONS

As usual, there are some objections (some of which will plague any version of event-causal libertarianism). The problem of luck rears its head again. Event-causal libertarians suggest that they do not share this problem with the simple indeterminists. Event-causalists, after all, are not suggesting that actions are uncaused. Thus, it is not a matter of luck that Brenda chooses to stay. It is, instead, caused by her reasons for staying. But opponents think there is still a problem of luck, due to the undetermined nature of this choice. Although Brenda's choice can be accounted for by things about Brenda just prior to her making it, nothing can explain why she chooses to stay rather than to go, since either option could occur. This seems to imply that her choice is a matter of luck. Thus, she cannot be held responsible for it.

Kane responds, in part, by suggesting that indeterminism need not detract from responsibility. For example, suppose that I want to break a window, so I throw a rock at it as hard as I can. Suppose further that it is undetermined whether the window will break. If the window does break, we don't then suggest that I am not morally responsible for breaking it. This is because I was *trying to break it*. We feel perfectly justified in holding someone responsible for doing something, even if it was undetermined whether she would succeed. Well, Brenda was trying to do what she did, either way. It does not matter that it was undetermined. Thus, she is responsible.

But the objector might note that Brenda's case is different from the rock through the window because in Brenda's case it is undetermined *which choice she will make*, not whether she will succeed at doing something she has chosen to do. Kane responds by noting that there is a difference between determining a choice right when it happens and determining it ahead of time. According to Kane, Brenda actually *determines* the outcome when she decides *by deciding*. It is just not *pre*determined by anything about her. Kane also emphasizes that it would be incorrect to think that Brenda makes her efforts and then chance takes over. This mistaken view would lend itself to the idea that it is a matter of luck what Brenda chooses. After all, if chance takes over after Brenda makes her efforts, Brenda has no control over the outcome. But Kane suggests that her efforts are being made the whole time until she determines the outcome by deciding.

Other objections concern these efforts themselves. Is it really possible to make competing efforts simultaneously? Clearly we can do more than one thing at a time, but can we try to do *conflicting* things at the same time? Even if it is possible, are we really responsible in such cases? And furthermore, don't these *efforts* need to be free so that Brenda is responsible? Suppose that it is, as Kane says, undetermined which effort of Brenda's will be successful. But suppose that her making these particular efforts is necessitated by something else. In other words, the outcome could be undetermined but the fact that she is trying each thing could be determined. Perhaps our evil neurosurgeon has manipulated her brain so that she would try to decide to stay and try to decide to go. This means that Brenda cannot help trying to make the decisions she is trying to make. How then, on an incompatibilist view, can she be responsible for her eventual choice? Kane supports his view by saying that we can be responsible for something because it is something we are trying to do. But doesn't he then need to add to his view that these efforts are freely made?

In response, Kane claims that Brenda is responsible for her efforts if they come from her character (rather than from an evil neurosurgeon!), since on his view her character comes from previous free choices (previous self-forming actions). They need not be undetermined themselves as long as they are coming from the person she has made herself into. Thus, through her previous free choices, Brenda has made herself into someone who cares about her career but who also cares about doing the right thing. She has created a person who has this particular conflict and makes these particular efforts when confronted with the situation on her way to the meeting. But the problem with this response is that there is a regress. In other words, won't we have to ask the same question about these previous self-forming actions and won't we eventually get to Brenda's earliest self-forming actions, which have no precursors? How will she be responsible for these earliest ones since they won't have come from a character that she has created? And if she is not responsible for these earliest ones, how is she responsible for all the subsequent ones?

Kane has an interesting response to this objection. He suggests that responsibility comes in degrees. Agents have very little responsibility for these earliest self-forming actions because they have not yet developed their characters very much. As they grow and develop, they build up a character and can be held more fully responsible for what they do.

These issues are still the subject of discussion and I will leave it to the reader to look into them. Although there are some important objections, Kane's view continues to be one of the most important and influential theories in the free will debate.

AGENT CAUSATION (OR AGENT-CAUSAL LIBERTARIANISM)

In order to understand this last libertarian view, we need to discuss some general issues concerning causation.

EVENT CAUSATION AND SUBSTANCE CAUSATION

The rock crushed the flower. The girl broke the vase. The water caused the soil to erode. These are all examples of causation. But so are these: the collision of one billiard ball with another caused the second to roll away. The sparking of the wire started the fire. The man's texting led to the car accident. What's the difference between the first set and the second? Well, the second set cites events as causes. The collision, the sparking, and the texting, are all events. The first set, however, cites what philosophers might call "substances". A "**substance**" in philosophical terminology is not the same as a "substance" in ordinary non-philosophical usage. In general, a substance in philosophical terms is an individual object or entity. Substances are distinguished from events and from properties (i.e. qualities or attributes). For example, "roundness", although an entity of sorts, is not a substance. A substance, such as a ball, has the property of roundness. And a collision, as cited in the example above, although a "thing", is not a substance either. It is an event, an occurrence, a happening. Although there is some philosophical controversy over exactly which things in the world should be counted as substances (and over whether there even are substances), for our purposes we can assume that ordinary objects, animals, persons, and stuffs (like water or acid) are substances.

Philosophers wonder which category of entity (events or substances) to cite as causes. Both categories seem like plausible candidates. And clearly, in ordinary parlance we cite both kinds of things, as I did at the beginning of this section. But nonetheless, many philosophers today think that substances are not really causes. These philosophers suggest that when we cite such substances, we are really speaking loosely. It is events involving these substances that are the causes. So, in saying that the rock crushed the flower, what we really mean is that *the event of the rock's rolling on top of the flower* is what crushed it. In suggesting that the girl broke the vase, this is shorthand for saying that *the event of her dropping it onto the tile floor* is what broke the vase. There are a number of reasons why these philosophers hold such a view. One important reason is that effects happen at particular times. The flower is crushed and the vase is broken at particular times. Substances tend to exist through many times (the rock and the girl exist over long periods of time). But events only happen at specific times. Thus, it seems to help explain the timing of an effect by citing an event as the cause.

There are important implications here for the free will debate. On the event-causal picture, if a human being causes something, her doing so entirely consists in certain mental events (which might be identical to or correlated with brain events). For example, suppose Tammy decides to tell the truth. This means that certain mental events, such as Tammy's thinking certain things, cause the decision. So perhaps right before deciding, Tammy deliberates and reasons that telling the truth is less likely to bring her regret. On this view, these mental events (or, perhaps on some views, brain events corresponding to these events) cause her decision. We can still say that Tammy causes the decision, but what we really mean more precisely is that mental events are doing so. This might sound like a trivial semantic issue. But it ends up making a more significant difference than you might suppose.

Most free will theorists today assume that events are what do the causing. As we saw with Robert Kane's view, for example, Brenda's efforts of will along with her reasons for making those efforts cause her decision. Likewise, most compatibilists hold that mental events are the direct causes of a person's free choices or actions.

But there is an alternative view. This view is called "agent causation" or "agent-causal libertarianism". According to agent causalists, events are not the most direct and primary causes of our free actions or choices. The view is called "agent causation", because its adherents claim that agents (i.e. persons), rather than events, do the causing, at least where free actions are concerned. Many of the current agent-causal views are inspired by historical philosophers such as Aristotle

(384–322 BCE) and Thomas Reid (1710–96 CE). Some theorists interpret Aristotle as claiming that agents can be the ultimate sources of a causal chain. Here is a famous Aristotelian example: a rock is moved by a staff, which is moved by a hand, which is moved by a man. They also see Aristotle as claiming that agents can serve as the ultimate answer to the question of how something was brought about. For example: What caused the accident? The woman in the red car.

Reid argues that genuine causation can only be attributed to things with **causal powers**. He claims that such powers can only be attributed to persons. Only persons can *do* things. Events happen, but they do not *do* anything. To cause is to *do*. Reid argues that real causal powers require something with a mind and intelligence, presumably because he thinks that only things with minds can exert their power. But what about effects like lightning storms that seem not to involve any person as cause? According to Reid, such effects *are* actually caused by a person – they are caused by God.

There are several recent agent-causal views. We will not be able to get into all the variations and details, but here is some information about such views. A famous theory explicated in the mid-twentieth century is Roderick Chisholm's view. Chisholm claims that there are two types of causation, one that applies to events and the other that applies to persons who can act intentionally and freely. He appeals to the example from Aristotle whereby the stone is moved by the staff, which is moved by the hand, which is moved by the man. He claims that in such an example, the man causes (via agent causation) the brain events that begin the action. The ensuing events then occur through event causation. In other words, the firing of nerves leading from the brain, and contraction of muscles occur via event-causal chains. A more recent view, offered by Timothy O'Connor, suggests that causation is best understood in terms of causal powers. On his view, lots of things have causal powers. But agents like us have special causal powers because we have special characteristics. This is somewhat like Reid's view, but O'Connor has a different account of causal powers. And he does not hold that only things with minds have them. Other things in the world have causal powers, but these powers are noticeably different from ours because other things in the world are not like us.

Some agent-causal views emphasize the difference between how we cause things and how events cause things. Other views suggest that there is really only one causal relation but it can hold between different kinds of things (i.e. substances and events). Randolph Clarke, for example, has suggested that if there is agent causation (though he doubts that there is), the relationship between an agent and the effect need not be any different from the relationship between an event and the effect.

Agent causalists claim that their view can solve the problem of free will by avoiding luck or randomness on the one hand, and determinism on the other. They believe that their view avoids the problem of luck because the agent, as a substance, determines the action. The simple indeterminist (like Ginet) and the event-causal libertarian (like Kane) are faced with explaining how the agent controls the action given that it is undetermined by the agent's reasons or anything else. Given the agent's reasons, it might happen or it might not. The agent causalist, on the other hand, can say that the agent determines the action. *She* makes it happen. It is not just that events inside of her might or might not lead to its occurrence. But the agent causalist claims that she avoids the worries concerning determinism, because nothing determines the action *other than the agent*. It is a libertarian view, so the idea is that determinism is false. (It should be noted, however, that there are some non-libertarian agent causalists. Ned Markosian, for example, argues for a compatibilist version of agent causation.) The agent avoids having her actions completely determined by the past and the laws of nature. Some agent causalists have thus called the agent an "undetermined determiner".

OBJECTIONS

At this point, it would be natural to wonder how agent causation is supposed to work. And although several notable philosophers (including those discussed above) have done a great deal to spell out the workings of agent causation, many other philosophers still object that it is too mysterious and inexplicable. They think that the causation we observe is generally event causation, so agent causation seems unusual. One response to this objection is to emphasize that event causation is not really as straightforward as it may seem. Thus, agent causalists may not have a special mystery to dispel. After all, philosophers are still engaged in heated debate about how best to understand and analyze event causation. All of the going theories of event causation suffer difficulties.

The next objection is one we have already seen when discussing simple indeterminism. This is a worry about reason explanations. If agents cause their actions, then it seems that reasons do not. While other views can have reasons corresponding to certain brain events that lead to decisions or actions, it seems that agent causation cannot have this. What this means is that the agent causalist, like the simple indeterminist, must have a non-causal account of reasons explanation. And it might seem problematic to understand how reasons explain without causing. But of course non-causalists do not see this as a problem at all. And so the debate continues.

One way to sidestep this worry about reasons comes from Randolph Clarke. He suggests that even with an agent-causal view, one could hold that reasons act as partial causes of one's action. Thus, the reasons will not determine the action, but they will causally influence it. The agent will then determine the action for those reasons. This is supposed to solve the worry about reason explanations because it can use reasons as causes.

Another famous objection to agent causation is the timing objection. As discussed earlier, because effects (including actions) occur at certain times, this feature seems best explained by the timing of the cause. But if the cause is not an event, then it is difficult to explain the timing. Suppose Prudence is 20 years old. She causes her hand to go up at 2:15 today. According to agent causation, the cause of the action is Prudence. Prudence has existed for 20 years, but the effect occurred only just now. How do we explain this? There are several responses but let's just focus on one here. If reasons are partial causes, as Clarke suggests, then there is no problem. That we come to have certain reasons at certain times can explain the timing of our actions, just as it would on an event-causal view.

As with all other theories, the debate over agent causation is ongoing. Some continue to argue that it is just too mysterious, or that it is just making up a name for something as a way of trying to explain it. Others hold that it would not really solve the problems it claims to solve. There would still be no way of explaining why an agent did one action rather than another, given that the agent could have performed either action. And others argue that the view, while coherent and able to solve the problems it claims to solve, is not scientifically supported or even plausible. But in any case, agent causation is a theory worth considering among the other solutions, all of which are themselves fraught with difficulties.

HARD DETERMINISM AND HARD INCOMPATIBILISM

Thus far, we have focused mainly on theories that attempt to preserve our free will and our moral responsibility. But now we must consider those theories that hold that we do not actually have free will (and that we are, thus, never responsible for what we do).

In Chapter 2, we discussed some of the reasons that someone might be an incompatibilist. Such a person might be convinced that determinism would rule out alternatives (and that alternatives are required for free will and responsibility). Or he might be convinced that since no one can do anything about the past and the laws of nature, then no one can do anything about what must follow from them. Since if determinism is true, everything (including actions) must follow from them, then no one can do anything about anything (the **Consequence Argument**)!

But why be a hard determinist or hard incompatibilist? As mentioned in Chapter 2, these positions deny our free will. A hard determinist believes that determinism is true. A hard incompatibilist, on the other hand, need not believe that determinism is true. But he thinks that either way, true or not, we cannot have free will. In general, those who deny our free will are convinced that conclusions from science and philosophy show that we cannot be free or responsible. Some of these philosophers argue that even if science seems to show that there is indeterminacy at the quantum level, there is not enough wiggle room at the level of actions. In other words, the fact that quantum particles do not always act predictably does not amount to any kind of freedom. Others argue that even if our actions are not deterministically caused, we still do not have free will because indeterministic causation is just as much a threat to freedom. We do not have any more control over these actions than we do over those which are deterministically caused. Derk Pereboom argues that only agent causation would allow for free will, since it would give us the ability to be the ultimate sources of our actions. But he claims that science rules out agent causation (or at least makes it highly implausible).

HOW IS THIS SUPPOSED TO SOLVE THE PROBLEM?

One might question how such views solve the problem of free will. In one sense, they do not solve the problem since we tend to see the problem as the problem of making room for free will. But on the other hand, they do settle the conflict. They just settle it in favor of the view that we do not have free will. Some of these thinkers lament the fact that we do not have free will. But others suggest that it is not really so bad. Pereboom, for example, argues that much of what we find meaningful in life is unthreatened by this conclusion that we lack free will and responsibility. Pereboom argues that there is still morality. Actions are still right and wrong even though no one is blameworthy or praiseworthy for them. For example, if Stella steals my computer, I can still judge that her action was morally wrong. I just can't blame her for stealing it because she was not the ultimate source of her action. And for her part, Stella cannot really feel guilty about what she has done, since she was not responsible. But she can, in a sense, regret that it happened. She can realize that it was wrong and hope to behave better in the future (though of course on this view it will not really be up to her how she will behave in the future!). Furthermore, Pereboom argues that our relationships are left intact even though we are not free and responsible. After all, we tend to love others not by choice, but due to other causes. I cannot help but love my children, for example. Why is this a problem? Pereboom argues that it is not. He also argues that there are significant benefits to his position. If we come to realize that others are not to blame, we will be less inclined to allow anger to overtake our judicious responses to wrongdoing. Instead of overreacting out of indignation, we will have a more balanced, pragmatic, and appropriate reaction.

OBJECTIONS

There are several ways one might object to such views. We cannot get into the details, but here are some general ways one might go about it. One might claim that the costs of such a view are much higher than Pereboom claims. This would not disprove the view itself, but it would undermine the claim about the view's implications. Another way to object would be to find flaws in the way such philosophers argue for their conclusion. For example, does the hard incompatibilist really establish that both determinism and indeterminism rule out responsibility? Others might question the claim that quantum indeterminacy does not amount to enough indeterminacy at the level of actions. And agent causalists might balk at Pereboom's claim that science has ruled out this possibility.

Once again, I leave it to the reader to pursue these issues. But hard determinism and hard incompatibilism are important views worth considering. And Pereboom's claims about the implications of such views are thought-provoking and important.

SUMMARY

Many notable philosophers argue that free will and moral responsibility cannot exist if determinism is true. Some of these philosophers believe that we are sometimes free and responsible. Others deny that we are ever free and responsible. Of those who think that we are sometimes free (and that determinism is false), some think our free actions are uncaused, some think that they are caused but not determined by mental events, and some think that they are agent-caused (caused by agents as substances rather than by mental events). Hard determinists and hard incompatibilists think we never have free will. Some of them suggest, however, that this should not trouble us as much as we think.

Recall the chart from Chapter 2. Here is a chart with just the incompatibilist views and some additional information from this chapter:

Table 5.1 Incompatibilist views

	Free Will	If Free Will, How Does it Occur?	Determinism
Simple Indeterminism	Yes	Uncaused basic mental action	No
Event-causal Libertarianism	Yes	Indeterministically caused by mental events	No
Agent-causal Libertarianism	Yes	Caused by the agent, as a substance	No
Hard Determinism	No	n/a	Yes
Hard Incompatibilism	No	n/a	It does not matter. We do not have the kind of free will required for responsibility in any case.

FURTHER READING

For a helpful overview of incompatibilist theories, see Randolph Clarke, "Incompatibilist (Nondeterministic) Theories of Free Will", in Edward N. Zalta (ed.), *The Stanford Encyclopedia of Philosophy* (Fall 2008 Edition), www.plato.stanford.edu/archives/fall2008/entries/incompatibilism-theories.

For more information and a helpful overview of the issues of action, including discussion of basic action and reasons, see George Wilson, "Action", in Edward N. Zalta (ed.), *The Stanford Encyclopedia of Philosophy* (Fall 2009 Edition), www.plato.stanford.edu/archives/fall2009/entries/action.

Anscombe and Davidson are two of the most important and influential sources for the debate over whether reasons are causes. Davidson argues that reasons must be causes. See Elizabeth Anscombe, *Intention*, reprint (Cambridge, MA: Harvard University Press, 2000); and Donald Davidson, *Essays on Actions and Events* (Oxford: Oxford University Press, 1980). Both are classic, highly important works on action.

For more recent discussion of reasons explanation, see Carl Ginet, "Reasons Explanations of Action: An Incompatibilist Account", *Philosophical Perspectives*, 3 (1989): 17–46; Carl Ginet, "Reasons Explanations of Action: Causalist versus Noncausalist Accounts", in Robert Kane (ed.), *The Oxford Handbook of Free Will* (New York: Oxford University Press, 2002), 386–405; and Timothy O'Connor and John Ross Churchill, "Reasons Explanation and Agent Control: In Search of an Integrated Account", *Philosophical Topics*, 32 (2004): 241–53.

For more on Carl Ginet's version of simple indeterminism, see Carl Ginet, *On Action* (Cambridge: Cambridge University Press, 1990); Carl Ginet, "Freedom, Responsibility, and Agency", *Journal of Ethics*, 1 (1997): 85–98; and Carl Ginet, "An Action Can Be Both Uncaused and Up to the Agent", in Christoph Lumer and Sandro Nannini (eds), *Intentionality, Deliberation and Autonomy: The Action-Theoretic Basis of Practical Philosophy* (Aldershot: Ashgate, 2007), 243–55.

For some other versions of simple indeterminism, see Stewart Goetz, "A Noncausal Theory of Agency", *Philosophy and Phenomenological Research*, 49 (1988): 303–16; Stewart Goetz, "Libertarian Choice", *Faith and Philosophy*, 14 (1997): 195–211; and Hugh McCann, *The*

Works of Agency: On Human Action, Will, and Freedom (Ithaca, NY: Cornell University Press, 1998).

For more on Robert Kane's version of event-causal libertarianism, see *The Significance of Free Will* (New York: Oxford University Press, 1996); and Robert Kane, "Responsibility, Luck, and Chance: Reflections on Free Will and Indeterminism", *Journal of Philosophy*, 96 (1999): 217–40. The latter provides some of Kane's responses to the problem of luck. Kane explains and defends his view against objections from three other prominent free will theorists in Robert Kane, "Libertarianism", in John Martin Fischer, Robert Kane, Derk Pereboom, and Manuel Vargas, *Four Views on Free Will* (Oxford: Blackwell, 2007), 5–43; and Robert Kane, "Response to Fischer, Pereboom, and Vargas", in John Martin Fischer, Robert Kane, Derk Pereboom, and Manuel Vargas, *Four Views on Free Will* (Oxford: Blackwell, 2007), 166–83. Kane also argues for his view in his excellent general introduction to free will. See Robert Kane, *A Contemporary Introduction to Free Will* (New York: Oxford University Press, 2005).

For other versions of event-causal libertarianism, see Laura Waddell Ekstrom, *Free Will: A Philosophical Study* (Boulder, CO: Westview Press, 2000); Laura Waddell Ekstrom, "Free Will, Chance, and Mystery", *Philosophical Studies*, 113 (2003): 153–80; Alfred R. Mele, *Autonomous Agents: From Self-Control to Autonomy* (New York: Oxford University Press, 1995); Alfred R. Mele, "Soft Libertarianism and Frankfurt-Style Scenarios", *Philosophical Topics*, 24(2) (1996): 123–41; Alfred R. Mele, "Ultimate Responsibility and Dumb Luck", *Social Philosophy & Policy*, 16 (1999): 274–93; and Alfred R. Mele, *Free Will and Luck* (New York: Oxford University Press, 2006). Ekstrom and Mele also have interesting and important contributions to the discussion of the problem of luck.

For an excellent general resource with entries on many important concepts, such as "substance", "event", "cause", and so on, see Helen Beebee, Nikk Effingham, and Philip Goff, *Metaphysics: The Key Concepts* (New York: Routledge, 2011). And for a good overview on "substance", see Howard Robinson, "Substance", in Edward N. Zalta (ed.), *The Stanford Encyclopedia of Philosophy* (Winter 2009 Edition), www.plato.stanford.edu/archives/win2009/entries/substance/.

For more on Thomas Reid and his agent-causal view, see Thomas Reid, [1788], *Essays on the Active Powers of the Human*

Mind (Cambridge, MA: MIT Press, 1969); and Gideon Yaffe and Ryan Nichols, "Thomas Reid", in Edward N. Zalta (ed.), *The Stanford Encyclopedia of Philosophy* (Winter 2009 Edition), www.plato.stanford.edu/archives/win2009/entries/reid/.

For Roderick Chisholm's agent-causal view, see "The Agent as Cause", in Myles Brand and Douglas Walton (ed.), *Action Theory* (Dordrecht: D. Reidel, 1976), 199–211; and "Human Freedom and the Self", in Gary Watson (ed.), *Free Will* (Oxford: Oxford University Press, 1982), 24–35.

For more current discussions of agent-causal libertarianism, see Randolph Clarke, "Toward a Credible Agent-Causal Account of Free Will", *Noûs*, 27 (1993): 191–203; Randolph Clarke, *Libertarian Accounts of Free Will* (New York: Oxford University Press, 2003); Timothy O'Connor, *Persons and Causes: The Metaphysics of Free Will* (New York: Oxford University Press, 2000); and Derk Pereboom, "Is Our Conception of Agent-Causation Coherent?", *Philosophical Topics*, 32 (2004): 275–86. It is worth noting that although they defend agent causation from a number of objections, Pereboom and Clarke are not themselves agent causalists. Pereboom thinks that agent causation is not scientifically possible and in his 2003 book, Clarke ends up arguing that agent causation, while coherent and able to withstand some of the bigger objections, is most likely not possible for other reasons. For a compatibilist version of agent causation, see N. Markosian, "A Compatibilist Version of the Theory of Agent Causation", *Pacific Philosophical Quarterly*, 80 (1999): 257–77.

For some defenses of hard determinism and hard incompatibilism, see Ted Honderich, *A Theory of Determinism: The Mind, Neuroscience, and Life Hopes*, 2 vols. (Oxford: Clarendon Press, 1988); Ted Honderich, "Compatibilism, Incompatibilism, and the Smart Aleck", *Philosophy and Phenomenological Research*, 66 (December 1996): 855–62; Ted Honderich, "Determinism as True, Both Compatibilism and Incompatibilism as False, and the Real Problem", in Robert Kane (ed.), *The Oxford Handbook of Free Will* (New York: Oxford, 2002), 461–76; Derk Pereboom, *Living Without Free Will* (Cambridge: Cambridge University Press, 2001); Derk Pereboom, "Hard Incompatibilism", in John Martin Fischer, Robert Kane, Derk Pereboom, and Manuel Vargas, *Four Views on Free Will* (Oxford: Blackwell, 2007), 85–125; and Galen Strawson, "The Impossibility of Moral Responsibility", *Philosophical Studies*, 75 (1994): 5–24.

6

OTHER POSITIONS

In the previous chapters, we've looked at different attempted solutions (or arguments that there are not solutions) to the problem of free will. These positions have been categorized in terms of **compatibilism** and **incompatibilism** and in terms of whether the views support free will and/or **determinism**. In this chapter, we will look at a few interesting and significant current views that tend not to fit as easily into these categories.

MYSTERIANISM

Human beings have a very strong drive to know and understand the world and their place in it. But some parts of our world or our experience seem to resist human comprehension. Some philosophers think that free will is one of these phenomena. Such a claim may seem almost trivial given the difficulties of coming to a solution to the problem of free will. After all, in each chapter, we've discussed major objections and pitfalls attending the various attempted solutions. But free will **mysterianism** is not just the claim that the problem of free will has yet to be solved (though this is certainly part of the view).

Peter van Inwagen argues for free will mysterianism. He claims that it might be that we are incapable of solving the problem of free will. Van Inwagen appeals to the arguments on both sides of the debate to illustrate how the problem is not (and perhaps cannot be) solved. On his view, there are successful arguments that free will is incompatible with determinism (e.g. the **Consequence Argument**). But there are also successful arguments that free will is incompatible with **indeterminism** (e.g. **the problem of luck**). So free will does not seem to be possible. Some philosophers agree with this and thus conclude that we should be hard incompatibilists and just admit that we cannot have free will. But van Inwagen thinks this is just as problematic, or maybe more so.

It is perhaps disturbing to us to think that we cannot have free will. But the mysterian is not just suggesting that it would be unfortunate if we did not have free will. The mysterian is suggesting that we cannot get rid of our belief in free will. Van Inwagen argues that in order to make a choice, one must deliberate between the options that one believes to be available. But I can't deliberate about whether to, say, go to class or whether to go to the movies if I do not think both of these options are actually possible for me. This kind of reasoning goes all the way back to Aristotle. Aristotle points out that deliberation is always about things in our own power (or at least about those things that we think are in our own power). I can't deliberate about whether two plus two equals four, or about who will win the big basketball game. Nor can I deliberate about what someone else is going to do. I can think about these things and construct reasoning and arguments to come to a conclusion. But this is not the same as what we do when we deliberate. The result of the math problem and the outcome of the basketball game are not in my power. Nor is what someone else will do. When I try to solve a math problem, I use reasoning to come to a conclusion about what is true. When I try to figure out who will most likely win the basketball game, I use the evidence available to make a prediction. When I think about what other people will or should do, I am not deliberating, even if I am thinking about what I would do in their shoes. I am reasoning through to a conclusion about what I think is best, or I'm culling evidence to come up with a prediction based on what I know of them. When I deliberate, on the other hand, my reasoning does not result in a theoretical truth or in a prediction. And while it does usually result in a judgment about what is best (as it might when I'm thinking about another person's choices), it also results in a choice. Van Inwagen's point is that deliberation, being a special kind of process, requires a belief in free will. So even those folks who deny free will in their philosophical musings, must actually believe in free will when it comes to going about their daily business.

The mysterian, then, argues that we cannot give up our belief in free will, but we also cannot figure out how it is possible, since it appears to be a contradictory phenomenon (it is incompatible with both determinism and indeterminism). He postulates that at least one of these incompatibility arguments must have a mistake somewhere, but it may not be possible for us to determine what it is.

HOW IS THIS SUPPOSED TO SOLVE THE PROBLEM (OR ISN'T IT)?

Obviously, unlike other positions we've discussed, mysterianism is more about highlighting the problem than it is about solving it. It is not attempting to resolve the problem of free will but is attempting to demonstrate how insoluble the problem really is. But it does offer some positive contributions. It might be of some comfort to the person who is convinced by the arguments of **hard incompatibilism**, for example, to think that the pull of these arguments may not prove that we cannot have free will. Perhaps our positive belief in free will is strong enough to withstand these arguments – not in the sense that it overcomes them, but in the sense that it does not crumble under their weight. Another virtue of the view is a refreshing kind of honesty and lack of philosophical hubris. In other words, there is something admirable about a view that plainly and openly admits that not everything is going to be comprehensible to us, but this does not mean that what is incomprehensible does not exist.

OBJECTIONS

It is probably not difficult to imagine what kinds of objections philosophers have to such a view. There are a number of different objections possible. One kind of objection is to argue that van Inwagen is wrong in thinking that there is incompatibility between either free will and determinism or between free will and indeterminism (or perhaps both!). We have already discussed these kinds of responses in considering the various compatibilist and incompatibilist views. Another objection would be to question why van Inwagen is so confident that we do have free will. There are two kinds of objections we might make here. First, we might wonder why our strong belief in free will needs to correspond with its actual existence. After all, people can have very strong and very durable beliefs in things that are not real or true. To be fair, van Inwagen is not fallaciously arguing that because we believe something, it must be true. His point is that those who argue against the existence of free will must have contradictory beliefs, because no one can really avoid believing in free will.

Second, we might question van Inwagen's claim that in order to deliberate, we must truly believe in free will. This is a complex issue. Van Inwagen claims that we must believe, while deliberating, that each option is possible for us. If we did not believe this, we could not seriously entertain each option. Furthermore, we could no longer see the point of deliberation as trying to reach a decision between our options. But perhaps van Inwagen is wrong about whether we need to believe that each option is possible. Philosopher Philip Pettit suggests that perhaps all that is needed is that *we fail to think an option is impossible*. There is a subtle difference here, but perhaps it is an important one. On the one hand, if we are determinists, we know that we can't do both options and that we will do one of them. In that sense, we know that one of them is impossible. But on the other hand, while deliberating, we don't know which one is impossible, so we can suspend beliefs about whether each one is possible or not. So while we are deciding, we cannot think any of our options in particular are impossible (we suspend belief on this score), but we do not need to actively believe that both of them are truly possible for us.

Derk Pereboom and others have suggested that part of what is required for deliberation to be possible for a determinist is that the determinist believe that her deliberations will be efficacious. In other words, a determinist can deliberate if, among other conditions, she believes that her deliberations will result in her doing the action that they point to (as being the best thing to do). So on this view, the determinist is able to deliberate because she believes that there is a genuine point to her deliberations. A belief in determinism need not make you think that your deliberations will not result in a choice. Thus, a choice is the outcome of deliberation for the determinist, just as it is for the non-determinist.

ILLUSIONISM

We now move from mystery to illusion. Mysteries and illusions may have some things in common, but they are quite different phenomena. On the one hand, they both seem to imply that there is some sort of underlying reality that does not readily present itself to us. On the other hand, there are important differences. An illusion need not be mysterious at all. Optical illusions, for example, are quite interesting, but not really mysterious. Scientists and those schooled in visual perception can explain why, for example, we see mirages on the hot pavement, or straight sticks that look bent under the water. And mysteries need not involve illusion. We might think it remains a mystery what really happened the day that JFK was assassinated, or that the construction of Stonehenge is utterly mysterious. But these need not involve any illusion (they could involve illusion but they need not in order to be mysterious).

Putting it very roughly, an illusion is when something appears to be one way, but really it is another. Free will **illusionism**, then, is going to involve this dichotomy between appearance and reality. But of course free will illusionism does not involve an optical illusion, but an illusion pertaining to our beliefs. Saul Smilansky is the main proponent (and creator) of this view. He claims that we have illusory beliefs about free will. He also claims that this is mostly a good thing.

But what are these illusory beliefs? One might naturally suppose that the illusory beliefs are that we have free will (when we really do not) and that we are sometimes morally responsible (when really we never are). These suppositions are not entirely wrong, but Smilansky's view is more complex than this. To understand his view, we need to talk a little bit about some of the standard views already discussed. Smilansky argues that libertarian free will is impossible (his reasons go along with the basic objections we've already discussed). He then argues that compatibilist accounts of free will are not sufficient. But the remaining possibility – **hard determinism** – is not fully acceptable either. Thus, Smilansky argues for an interesting combination. Although we normally see compatibilism and hard determinism as mutually exclusive, Smilansky argues that compatibilism and hard determinism are both true in important ways. We need to be partly compatibilists and partly hard determinists, and we need to try to integrate these views' respective insights.

Smilansky thinks that hard determinism is problematic on its own, because it does not allow us to make moral distinctions between cases that seem to require them. In other words, if everyone is determined, then we cannot say that a common thief is more in control and responsible than a full-blown kleptomaniac (who presumably has a psychological compulsion to steal). We want to be able to distinguish between these cases for ethical reasons, both because there are real distinctions here, and because people and societies can't function well without assuming and accepting **moral responsibility**. Compatibilism allows us to do so because compatibilist accounts can distinguish between agents who lack any sort of control (e.g. the kleptomaniac) and those who have what he calls "local control" over their actions (e.g. the common thief). Since everyone would want to be free of oppressive compulsions like kleptomania, even under determinism, this shows that determinism is not the only thing that matters, and that there are important senses of control or free will that are compatible with determinism.

But compatibilism is not sufficient for other moral reasons. For example, compatibilism seems to ignore the fact that if determinism is true, no one is the ultimate source of action. If determinism is true, then I might have local control over my action, but from a broader perspective, my action has its *ultimate* source well before my birth. The common thief may have controlled his action locally, for example, through his own reasons, desires, and so on, but these reasons and desires and his character ultimately trace back to factors over which the thief has no control. And if determinism is true, this is the case for everyone. Thus, no one is deeply responsible and it is therefore wrong to hold anyone to be deeply responsible and to punish anyone as if deeply responsible. Smilansky argues that compatibilism is morally "shallow" because it does not recognize that from a broader or higher perspective (what he calls "the ultimate perspective") we should notice that determined agents are not truly the sources of their actions in the way required for deep responsibility. Compatibilism also does not acknowledge the unfairness of punishing or blaming someone who is not the ultimate source of action.

Smilansky goes on to argue that it is crucial for the functioning of civil society that we maintain a belief in free will. He thinks this is crucial because (in most cases at least), people need to believe they are free and will be held responsible in order to feel remorse and in order to be motivated to do the right thing. And only a social order that respects agency and broadly follows compatibilist distinctions (which he calls a "Community of Responsibility") will truly respect persons. Moreover, we need to believe we are free in order to have a deep sense of value and achievement in both moral matters and other meaningful elements of our lives. But compatibilist free will isn't good enough for the reasons already discussed.

So what are we to do? In some ways, we are to continue doing what we have been doing. Smilansky's suggestion is that we do in fact have illusory beliefs about free will and that this is a good thing. We do tend to think of ourselves as libertarian agents – those who act freely in an incompatibilist (libertarian) sense. And as long as we ignore the "ultimate perspective", we can maintain this illusory libertarian belief. We can think of ourselves as libertarian agents because we are not thinking about the looming dangers of determinism. We in fact often have a kind of compatibilist free will (that is, we often have "local control" over our actions and are responsible in a "shallow" sense), but we believe in and ought to believe in a more robust libertarian freedom. On the other hand, Smilansky implies that we should not completely forget about the ultimate perspective and about hard determinism. It is important, for example, that those who dole out punishments remember that ultimately, no one has any control over the actions that are performed.

HOW IS THIS SUPPOSED TO SOLVE THE PROBLEM?

With this view, as with mysterianism, there is not a theoretical "solution" if by that we mean a resolution in favor of full-fledged freedom and responsibility. But unlike mysterianism, illusionism does suggest a practical solution. We can supposedly preserve what is important to us in our daily lives and in our relationships with others through the continued belief in the illusion of libertarian free will (as long as there is no widespread public awareness that it is an illusion).

OBJECTIONS

There are a number of potential objections here. Some of the objections will center on whether Smilansky is really correct that compatibilism or hard determinism have the implications he claims.

Is compatibilist free will really "shallow"? Must we be the ultimate source of our actions in order to be deeply responsible? (John Fischer argues that the answers to these questions is "no". He thinks that the "ultimate perspective" is too far away and not the important perspective that we need to take up in order to understand responsibility.) Does a belief in hard determinism really undermine our relationships, feelings of worth, and motivation to do the right thing? Someone like Pereboom (whose view is discussed in Chapter 5) will say no. Libertarians will question whether the view really is impossible in the way he suggests (the libertarians discussed in Chapter 5 would presumably balk at this suggestion). Other potential objections might center on the value and possibility of illusory beliefs.

I leave it to the interested reader to pursue these issues further. But in any case, illusionism is an interesting and important position to think about in the context of the debate.

REVISIONISM

The free will debate is notoriously tricky for a number of reasons. One reason it is so difficult is that philosophers seem to disagree about how exactly to characterize free will. There are a number of disputes about what our concept of free will really is (one dispute, for example, involves whether our concept includes alternative possibilities). A relatively recent suggestion, however, is that our current conception is one thing but it ought to be something else. Manuel Vargas espouses a new view called "**revisionism**". He argues that the proper philosophical theory of free will requires us to revise our concept of what free will is.

We all know what it means to revise a paper. But what does it mean to revise a concept? Perhaps revising a concept isn't all that different from revising a paper. When you revise a paper, you look for elements that do not fit and you cross them out. You might rearrange sections and add things as well. Some papers require more revisions than others and some papers look drastically different after revision, while others are basically the same. But in every case, we start with one thing and alter it according to some sort of standard. As with paper revision, with concept revision, we may also "cross out" elements that do not fit. Vargas gives examples of concepts that have been revised. For example, he suggests that "marriage" used to denote property exchange. But today we can refer to something as a marriage and we do not mean it to include an exchange of property. This part of the concept has been crossed out. Or we can say that David Blaine is a "magician", without meaning that we believe him to have supernatural powers (as the concept used to entail). We also sometimes add to a concept. Our concept of water, for example, now includes its molecular structure. This has been added to the concept.

We revise a paper in order to make it better in some sense. Likewise, we revise a concept to make it better. But better how? In general, concept revision happens because we want our concepts to be *accurate*. We want them to reflect the world as we know it. Our concept of marriage no longer includes property exchange because it is no longer accurate to say that marriages center on property exchange. Thus, if the concept of free will needs to be revised, it's because the concept is no longer accurate. As with other concepts, if we now know more about free will, we need to revise our concept to match our understanding.

Vargas' particular version of revisionism is based on the claim that our original concept (our "rough draft" if you will forgive the continued analogy) of free will is incompatibilist (libertarian). In other words, we commonly think of free will in terms of having genuine alternative possibilities – the kind that are incompatible with determinism. Vargas gives several interesting and compelling arguments for why he thinks this, but we cannot get into these here. Suffice it to say that he begins with the idea that this is our concept, or at least part of it, and then he suggests revision.

Vargas argues that we need to revise this libertarian concept because it is unlikely, scientifically speaking. It seems unlikely, for instance, that we have indeterministic processes happening in our brains at just the right times in just the right ways. Furthermore, if we do not have this kind of agency, then we run into major problems with moral responsibility. In other words, this incompatibilist concept of free will says it's unfair to hold someone responsible unless certain precarious incompatibilist conditions occur. This means that we are probably often unfairly holding people accountable.

Thus, Vargas advocates that our concept be revised to a compatibilist concept. I will not go into the details of his compatibilism, but very roughly, he advocates a view whereby agents are sensitive to moral reasons and are able to act in accordance with such considerations.

HOW IS THIS SUPPOSED TO SOLVE THE PROBLEM?

Revisionism claims to solve the problem of free will in a different way. It allows for the existence of free will because it suggests that we revise our concept to fit the evidence we have about the way the world really is. Free will turns out to be different than what we thought it was, but this is okay. Light and sound have turned out to be different than we originally thought they were as well. New knowledge about light, for example, did not mean that we were wrong in thinking light existed. It just meant that light was not quite what we had thought. New knowledge and understanding lead to revised concepts that enable a kind of coherence and accuracy about the world. Vargas emphasizes that what we want from a concept of free will is a way of knowing when it is appropriate to judge someone praiseworthy or blameworthy. This is what free will and responsibility are *for*. A properly revised concept will allow us to maintain our ability to hold people responsible because it will have been revised with this in mind.

OBJECTIONS

Let's discuss a few objections that apply to the specific version of revisionism laid out here. The first objection to note is that perhaps our original concept of free will is not in fact an incompatibilist concept. If that's true, then Vargas is wrong in saying that our concept needs to be revised. If our concept is already compatibilist, then no revision is required. Another objection is that a compatibilist conception is not a more accurate conception. Vargas argues that we should revise to a compatibilist conception because such a conception is more accurate. Incompatibilists will obviously resist that conclusion. I will leave it to the interested reader to look into these objections and potential replies.

A third objection, which I will discuss briefly, is that revisionism is not really a unique view. The idea is that all compatibilist views employ revision. But Vargas thinks that his view is importantly different and that it has an important advantage over typical compatibilist views. Other compatibilist views tend to argue that people don't *really* think of agency in incompatibilist terms – that if people follow the compatibilist arguments to their logical conclusions, they will see that their intuitions really point in another direction. But Vargas sees this as implausible. Instead, he suggests that people really in fact think of agency in incompatibilist terms, but that they should get rid of the incompatibilist elements of the free will concept. Other compatibilists commonly claim that if we clarify our beliefs, we will come to see that they are actually compatibilistic. In other words, the typical compatibilist is suggesting that we should line up what we really think with what we tend to say when we are not thinking clearly. But Vargas is suggesting something stronger than this. He is suggesting that we should actually change *what we think* about free will. Vargas contends that this is an important difference.

This relatively new view has already garnered lots of attention and spurred lots of debate. It is a subtle, complex, and important contender in the free will debate.

SUMMARY

In this chapter, we looked at positions that do not fall into the typical compatibilist/incompatibilist categories. But each view is an important alternative to consider when thinking about free will. Mysterianism is the view that we cannot seem to get rid of our belief in free will, but we also cannot figure out how to support this belief (since there are good arguments to show that it is incompatible with both determinism and indeterminism). Illusionism suggests that we ought to maintain the illusory belief that we have libertarian free will, even though such is not possible. And revisionism suggests that we ought to revise our concept of free will to something that is more accurate.

FURTHER READING

For van Inwagen's arguments as to why free will is a mystery, see Peter van Inwagen, "The Mystery of Metaphysical Freedom", in Peter van Inwagen and Dean W. Zimmerman (eds), *Metaphysics: The Big Questions* (Oxford: Blackwell, 1998), 365–74; and Peter van Inwagen, "Free Will Remains a Mystery", *Philosophical Perspectives*,

14 (2000): 1–19. For some responses, see Laura Waddell Ekstrom, "Free Will, Chance, and Mystery", *Philosophical Studies*, 113 (2003): 153–80; and Meghan Griffith, "Does Free Will Remain a Mystery? A Response to van Inwagen", *Philosophical Studies*, 124 (2005): 261–69.

For more on the issue of whether deliberation is possible when one believes in determinism, see Derk Pereboom, "A Compatibilist Account of the Epistemic Conditions on Rational Deliberation", *The Journal of Ethics*, 12 (2008): 287-307; and Philip Pettit, "Determinism with Deliberation", *Analysis*, 49(1) (1989): 42–44.

For more on Saul Smilansky's illusionism, see Saul Smilansky, *Free Will and Illusion* (Oxford: Oxford University Press, 2000); and Saul Smilansky, "Free Will, Fundamental Dualism, and the Centrality of Illusion", in Robert Kane (ed.), *The Oxford Handbook of Free Will*, 2nd edition (Oxford: Oxford University Press, 2011), 425–41. For an objection to Smilansky's claims about the ultimate perspective and ultimate sourcehood, see John Martin Fischer, "Sourcehood: Playing the Cards That are Dealt You", in Fischer, *Deep Control* (Oxford: Oxford University Press, 2012), 163–85.

For more on Manuel Vargas' revisionism, see Manuel Vargas, "The Revisionist's Guide to Responsibility", *Philosophical Studies*, 125 (2005): 399–429; Manuel Vargas, "Revisionism about Free Will: A Statement and Defense", *Philosophical Studies*, 144(1) (2009), 45–62; and Manuel Vargas, "Revisionist Accounts of Free Will: Origins, Varieties, and Challenges", Robert Kane (ed.), *The Oxford Handbook of Free Will*, 2nd edition (Oxford: Oxford University Press, 2011), 457–74. Vargas discusses his view and responds to three other prominent free will theorists in: John Martin Fischer, Robert Kane, Derk Pereboom, and Manuel Vargas, *Four Views on Free Will* (Malden, MA: Blackwell Publishers, 2007).

7

FREE WILL AND SCIENCE

In recent years, the scientific community has been weighing in on the issue of free will. Many articles in scientific journals and in popular science venues discuss the implications of scientific research for whether we have free will. Some of these articles talk about quantum physics, some about neuroscience, and some discuss experiments with other animals (fruit flies even!).

Most current-day philosophers agree that science is relevant to the free will issue in various ways. After all, physicists can give us insight into whether **determinism** is true. And psychologists and neuroscientists will have a lot to tell us about our motivations and our brain processes. But when scientists conclude that their experiments prove the existence or non-existence of free will, are such conclusions justified? In this chapter, we will discuss the role science may have to play in the issue of free will.

DETERMINISM AND SCIENCE

Historically, the question of whether determinism is true or false was the matter of philosophical debate. Now, however, philosophers are often willing to defer to the scientists on this question. But there are still some philosophical issues here. Quantum mechanics is often said to be indeterministic. The behavior of quantum-level particles seems probabilistic – that is, scientists cannot predict exactly the way these particles will behave. They can only assign probabilities. Certain phenomena such as radioactive decay and photon emission are examples of ultimately unpredictable quantum behavior. Suppose scientists have a bit of radium. The scientists cannot determine when a given atom will decay. They can only assign probabilities for how much of the radium will decay over a certain temporal interval. Many scientists and philosophers assume that this means that the world is not deterministic. But some scientists and philosophers suggest that there could be hidden variables. They think that if we had all the information, we would be able to predict what quantum particles would do. So perhaps the quantum world is deterministic after all, but we just need a better theory. Thus, there are different interpretations of quantum mechanics, some of which are indeterministic and some of which are deterministic. Both scientists and philosophers should weigh in on this debate.

QUANTUM PHYSICS AND THE HUMAN BRAIN

Suppose that quantum physics is indeed indeterministic. Libertarians sometimes view this information as supporting their view of free will. But other philosophers have objected that quantum-level **indeterminism** does not end up amounting to macro-level indeterminism. In other words, just because a single atom may not behave deterministically, this does not mean that neurons, which are composed of many molecules (and thus even more atoms), will behave indeterministically. On the bigger level, maybe indeterminism does not amount to much and things are pretty well determined. Here's an analogy. Think of the tiny pixels that compose a digital picture. Suppose, for the sake of the analogy, that the behavior of each pixel is somewhat random in that there is no way to predict whether it will burn out or not. But suppose further that it is predictable that only a small percentage of the total pixels will burn out. Although the pixels compose the picture, their random activity does not really affect the overall picture.

But there are responses that the libertarian can make here – responses grounded in modern physics. Some philosophers have suggested that something called **chaos theory** could make libertarian free will more likely. Chaos theory, very roughly, is the idea that certain systems are such that very small changes in the system can produce much larger effects. One common way of thinking of this is the so-called "butterfly effect". If a particular butterfly in Argentina flaps its wings, this could, through a chain of causes, lead to a tornado three weeks later in Texas. A very small event, very far away, gets amplified and leads to large effects. The libertarian might suggest that if there is chaos, then very small quantum indeterminacies might be amplified to produce big effects on the neuronal level. And if the brain is itself chaotic, the firing of a single neuron could be amplified to produce bigger effects. Robert Kane, whose view we discussed in Chapter 5, mentions chaos as lending scientific plausibility to his libertarian view.

The use of chaos theory, while exciting and worth considering, is also the target of some further objections. For example, scientists do not agree on whether there is chaos in the brain. It is a very difficult empirical matter that may not be decided upon for a long time. Furthermore, even if brain processes involve indeterminism, it is difficult to know whether this helps us. Does the indeterminism function in just the right way and at just the right time for us to be able to utilize it to produce an action? Or does it just provide some randomness to our behavior?

These scientific issues obviously have an important bearing on certain views of free will. They are not the whole story, of course. Philosophers play a crucial role in looking at the scientific evidence and teasing out its implications.

UNPREDICTABLE FRUIT FLIES?

It might sound a bit comical to think that fruit flies could tell us anything about free will. But there is an interesting study that purports to do just that. Philosophers, however, may question whether the study tells us what the scientists claim that it does.

Scientists took fruit flies and tethered them in a white container. The idea was to make it so that the flies were getting no input from their environment. Furthermore, because they were tethered, the flies' ability to turn left or right did not really get them anywhere. It did not give them any kind of positive or negative feedback. The researchers looked at the flies' behavior (which way they would turn). They found that the flies' behavior was not random. The researchers determined this by comparing the flies' behavior to various computer simulations that model randomness. This is an interesting result, because it might have been supposed that in the absence of external input, the flies would have just behaved randomly. The study is supposed to show, then, that the flies are able to behave both spontaneously and non-randomly. Their behavior is spontaneous because it is not entirely the result of external input, and it is non-random based on the computer comparison. Furthermore, the scientists suggest that their study provides evidence of indeterministic processes in the flies' brains. Scientists theorize about the evolutionary advantages of indeterministic brain processes. Among other things, they suggest that such processes would make behavior unpredictable and therefore make animals harder to capture as prey. The researchers do not claim that flies have free will in the same way that we might (if we do). But they claim that an ability to behave spontaneously in a non-random way could show some sort of biological grounding for free will.

Such results could be of interest to philosophers studying free will. But philosophers will urge anyone making claims about free will to get clear on what is meant by free will. For instance, is it an incompatibilist notion or a compatibilist one? Notice that there appears to be an assumption that free will requires an absence of determination. This sounds like they are assuming an incompatibilist notion. Compatibilist philosophers will obviously balk at this. On the other hand, the scientists do seem to assume that randomness would rule out free will, a conclusion that most philosophers would agree with. There are lots of issues here and scientists and philosophers would do well to discuss them with one another.

FREE WILL AND PSYCHOLOGY

PSYCHOLOGICAL DETERMINISM

Here is a true story. I was once engaged in a nice conversation with a psychologist. I was discussing my research interests – free will and human action. The psychologist then commented that we have no free will because our decisions and choices are entirely the product of psychological forces. End of story. This psychologist was completely confident that some kind of determinism is true and was also confident that this kind of determinism is incompatible with free will. It is my understanding that not all psychologists necessarily agree with these claims. But there is certainly a tendency in psychology (and in general) to think of human behavior as determined by both internal and external psychological factors. Sometimes philosophers will distinguish **psychological determinism** from causal/nomological determinism. Psychological determinism is, roughly, the view that our behavior is determined by our psychology. Notice that this could be true even if causal determinism is false. There could be indeterminacy in the world, but our behavior could still be necessitated by our psychology.

Certainly, psychological determinism is intuitively plausible. It does seem that our current behavior is based in large measure on what has happened to us in the past or on certain psychological features that we have inherited or otherwise acquired. Philosophers ought to take seriously the empirical data that psychologists have collected pertaining to such issues. But it is worth pointing out that a view like psychological determinism will be difficult to prove empirically. In order to prove that a person's behavior has been necessitated, we would need a "control". We would need to know whether the person could have done otherwise, even given the same psychological background. It is not clear how we could do this. Psychologists can collect data from lots of different human subjects and see that certain similar backgrounds predict certain similar behaviors, but this is not the same thing as proving that these behaviors are necessitated by the backgrounds.

FREE WILL AND NEUROSCIENCE

Perhaps the biggest headlines with respect to free will and science come from experiments in neuroscience. Some neuroscientists have gone so far as to claim that neuroscience proves the absence of free will. Philosophers are skeptical.

LIBET EXPERIMENTS

The most famous neuroscience experiment to stir up debate concerning free will was conducted by Benjamin Libet in the 1980s. Libet-style experiments have been repeated since that time.

For his experiment, Libet used electrodes on the scalps of his subjects in order to detect something called the Readiness Potential or RP. The Readiness Potential is an electrical change occurring in the brain. It had previously been shown to occur about a second before certain types of voluntary bodily movements. For his new experiment, Libet instructed his subjects to flex or flick their wrists whenever they felt like doing so. He asked the subjects to look at a fast-moving clock and report the time at which they first became aware of the urge to flick. When a subject flexed, the computer recorded the time that the muscles began to contract, along with the time at which there was an electrical change (the RP). These two things, along with the subject's report of the time at which there was first awareness of the urge to move, gave Libet a kind of timeline for action. Here is what he found. Approximately 550 milliseconds before the muscle movement there was an RP onset. Subjects reported that they first noticed the urge to move at about 200 milliseconds before the movement. (Libet performed other experiments that corrected this time to be 150 milliseconds before the movement. Subjects were given a skin stimulus and asked to recall and report the time at which they noticed it. They were off by about 50 milliseconds.) Here is what that timeline looks like:

−550 ms   −200 ms (−150 ms)   0 ms

RP onset   awareness of urge   muscle movement

This timeline might seem to have the following troubling implication with regard to free will. It seems that although subjects thought they were acting freely, their actions actually began well before they were even aware of them. If my decision has been made and my action is underway before I even realize that I've decided to perform it, how can I have any control over it? Thus, how can I be acting freely?

Libet concluded from his study that we do not have any positive kind of free will. But interestingly, he hypothesized that we may have what some have referred to as "free won't". This is a kind of veto power over actions that are already underway. Subjects in his experiments reported having urges to move that they did not subsequently act upon. It seemed that they were able to veto such actions and thereby stop them from occurring.

RESPONSES TO LIBET

Upon hearing about this experiment, many people question the accuracy of subjects' reports about when they felt the urge to move. And there may be some reason to question this. But I will set this sort of objection aside since that is an objection pertaining to the parameters of the experiment. Instead, I'd like to focus on certain philosophical objections.

MELE'S OBJECTIONS TO LIBET

Notable philosopher Alfred Mele has responded in detail to these and other neuroscience experiments. Here are some of his concerns.

WHAT IS REALLY HAPPENING AT −550 MS?

First, Mele questions Libet's interpretation of his results. Libet implies that RP onset is correlated with some sort of unconscious decision or intention to move. Libet thinks that this means that we are essentially making decisions before we are aware of them; therefore we are not free. Mele suggests, alternatively, that RP onset could correlate with any number of things. It could be some sort of precursor to an intention. It could be a cause of an intention rather than an intention itself. This is important because it may not be problematic to think that our intentions have causes (you will recall that most of the free will theories we've discussed allow for a causal chain).

Mele then provides experimental evidence that his hypothesis is more plausible. He uses reaction time experiments to support his hypothesis over Libet's. If Libet is correct, then it seems that it takes approximately 550 milliseconds for an intention to lead to a muscle movement. But reaction time experiments show that it takes considerably less time to go from intention to muscle movement. In a different experiment, subjects were told to push a button upon hearing a signal. This tested their reaction time. Reaction times were around 231 milliseconds. What this means is that subjects were able to detect the signal, form an intention to press the button, and then move their fingers to press it, all much more quickly than 550 milliseconds. The length of time between intention and movement was probably much closer to the length of time between the awareness of the urge and the movement in Libet's experiment.

FALLACIOUS REASONING ABOUT FREE WILL

Mele also discusses certain fallacious arguments that have been made based on Libet's experiments. Some scientists have claimed that because conscious intention occurs after the RP onset, conscious intention therefore plays no role in our actions. But as Mele points out, this reasoning makes no sense. Just because there is something in the causal chain that is prior to conscious intention, this does not prove that conscious intention is not also causally efficacious. Mele draws the following analogy. Suppose that you light the fuse on a firecracker, the fuse burns, then the firecracker explodes. You wouldn't say that because the burning of the fuse occurs after the lighting of the fuse, the burning plays no role in the firecracker's exploding. Just because there is an earlier element in the causal chain, it does not mean that a later element has no causal role to play.

WHAT BEARING DO THESE STUDIES HAVE ON MORE COMPLEX DECISIONS?

Mele also discusses the relationship between the kinds of decisions that are made when participating in a Libet-type experiment and other kinds of decisions. Libet cases, argues Mele, are cases that involve the **liberty of indifference**. Such cases arise when an agent is indifferent about his top alternatives. If I am at the grocery store and I have chicken soup on my list, I will most likely be indifferent about which of two perfectly good cans I pick up and put in my cart. Picking one of the cans of soup over another is akin to picking one time to flick one's wrist over another time.

The reason this is relevant is that most of our free choices, if we have them, are probably not cases of the liberty of indifference. So any results from these experiments cannot be extended to other kinds of cases. Mele also points out that in other kinds of decisions, we are often aware of the causes of these decisions. If I decide to buy a house, for example, I am presumably aware of some of the causes of this decision. I will be aware of the kind of reasoning I used in my deliberations and to back up my eventual choice. But with the liberty of indifference cases, it is more plausible that I might not always be aware of the causes of my decisions. So, perhaps I am not aware of why I pick the can of soup on the left rather than on the right. Likewise, if I am a subject in a Libet experiment, I may not be aware of the causal precursors to my conscious intention to flex my wrist. This should not worry us. These causal precursors are just not generally important enough for us to be aware of them.

Finally, Mele emphasizes again that we should not be bothered by the idea that our decisions or intentions have causes. So even if the process which culminates in my action begins up to 550 milliseconds before, this should be no cause for concern. This just means that my actions do not come out of nowhere. The only free will view that might be ruled out, then, is **simple indeterminism** since the simple indeterminist insists that my action must be uncaused. But most of the philosophical positions on free will can accommodate the idea that our actions are caused.

Notice that Libet's experiments do not show that the causal precursor (RP onset) necessitates the occurrence of the action. In fact, Libet himself implies the denial of this, by claiming that we have a veto power. In other words, the RP onset does not mean that the action has to follow. It may follow or it may not. It could be that RP onset is *required* for the subsequent action, but that should not bother anyone. If I want to drive to Tuscaloosa, I must get into a vehicle. But that doesn't mean that getting into a vehicle forces me to go to Tuscaloosa. Getting into a vehicle is required, but it's not the whole story. Likewise, perhaps the RP onset is required for the action, but it does not necessitate the action.

IS CONSCIOUS WILL AN ILLUSION?

Psychologist Daniel Wegner has argued that conscious will is not real. We think we are consciously causing our actions through our intentions, but really, such feelings of conscious will are just add-ons. According to Wegner, our thoughts and actions can be connected, but our feeling of will – our feeling that we are intentionally causing our actions – is something that arises as we try to interpret what is going on. To get at this idea, Wegner gives examples whereby thoughts lead directly to action without our having the experience of willing. This kind of phenomenon is called "ideomotor action". One example of ideomotor action is "table turning". Imagine a group of people with their hands on a table, waiting for a spirit to communicate with them in some sort of séance. Often in such scenarios, the table will start moving and many of the participants will honestly believe that they have nothing to do with it. Presumably, they are in fact moving the table, but supposedly there is no intention or willing involved (this is similar to what happens when people use a Ouija board). Their thoughts and expectations about its moving are leading to the action, but not through any kind of intention or will – or so Wegner argues.

Thus, ideomotor theory suggests that thoughts lead directly to action, but it is not through any kind of intention or will. It is as if we, as agents, are cut out of the picture. Wegner appears to be suggesting that all actions are really like this, and the only difference is that with some actions the illusion of conscious will arises. In the cases in which we do not have the illusion, it is because something has gotten in the way of the process. When we do have the illusion of will, the general idea is that our feeling of willing is just our way of interpreting what's going on behind the scenes. We are not really acting, we just feel as if we are. We sort of retrospectively interpret what's going on as being our own doing.

But as Mele and others point out, it seems strange to suppose that just because there are some ideomotor actions, that therefore all actions function the same way. Why assume that intentional actions are just like ideomotor actions except with an illusion tacked on? Why suppose that when I am undergoing a complex process of deliberation and decision-making that the intention I eventually form has absolutely no causal result? As philosopher Eddy Nahmias suggests, why would such processes of deliberation and intention have evolved if they were just going to allow us to look at our actions after the fact and just feel as if we intended them? Alternatively, Mele also suggests that with something like "table turning", for example, there may very well be an intention or willing causing the action. It may just not be fully conscious. (Mele argues that there seems to be good reason to believe that we sometimes unconsciously intend things. For example, experienced drivers often turn on their turn signals without being fully aware of doing so. They most likely have unconscious intentions to do so.)

To further support the idea that intentions do causal work, Mele cites experiments concerning what are called "implementation intentions". Implementation intentions are basically plans for how you are going to carry out some longer-term goal. In several different psychology experiments, it was shown that implementation intentions have very strong causal results. For example, in one study, all participants had expressed strong intentions to perform a breast self-examination during the next month. One group was told to write down some implementation intentions – that is, to specify where and when they would perform them. The control group was not asked to do so. Only 53 percent of the control group performed the self-exams, whereas 100 percent of the other group performed them. Mele argues that these experiments provide very strong evidence that intentions (in this case the implementation intentions) have causal efficacy. These intentions obviously led to different results because those who did not form these intentions were much less likely to perform the self-exam.

It seems then, that there is good reason to believe that conscious will is not, in general, an illusion.

SUMMARY AND CONCLUSION

In this chapter, we discussed some of the scientific theories and experiments that might have bearing on free will. We discussed things like quantum physics and whether it is deterministic and whether it allows for libertarian free will. Does quantum indeterminacy (if it exists) really give us what we need for libertarian free will? Can studies of animal brains tell us anything about whether free will is a natural process built into our brains? We also discussed psychology and neuroscience and what kinds of issues these fields raise for our understanding of free will. Are we psychologically determined? Does neuroscience show that we "decide" what to do before we are aware of making a decision? Or is it just that in cases of the liberty of indifference, some causal precursor to action begins before we are aware of it? Is conscious will an illusion, or does the evidence not really support this claim?

Obviously, then, there are many scientific issues that have bearing on free will. But it is important to note that in every case, the philosophical issues need to be attended to. We need to use philosophical reasoning and argument to understand the concepts involved – concepts such as free will, intention, consciousness, and so on. And philosophers are in a good position to discuss the implications of scientific research for issues like free will and **moral responsibility**. But philosophers also need to pay attention to the scientific evidence as well. Regardless of whether we are wholly physical, we know that we are at least partly physical. We are also subject to various psychological forces. This means that we need to incorporate what psychologists and scientists have to say about how we function.

FURTHER READING

For a helpful overview of chaos theory, see Robert Bishop, "Chaos", in Edward N. Zalta (ed.), *The Stanford Encyclopedia of Philosophy* (Fall 2009 Edition), www.plato.stanford.edu/archives/fall2009/entries/chaos/. For more on how this relates to free will, see Robert Bishop, "Chaos, Indeterminism, and Free Will", in Robert Kane (ed.), *Oxford Handbook of Free Will*, 2nd edition (New York: Oxford University Press, 2011), 84–100.

For some general information about causal determinism, see Carl Hoefer, "Causal Determinism", in Edward N. Zalta (ed.), *The Stanford Encyclopedia of Philosophy* (Spring 2010 Edition), www.plato.stanford.edu/archives/spr2010/entries/determinism-causal/.

For more on the relation between quantum physics and free will, see David Hodgson, "Quantum Physics, Consciousness, and Free Will", in Robert Kane (ed.), *Oxford Handbook of Free Will*, 2nd edition (New York: Oxford University Press, 2011), 57–83.

The study on the fruit flies can be found here: A. Maye, C-h. Hsieh, G. Sugihara, B. Brembs (2007) "Order in Spontaneous Behavior", *PLoS ONE* 2(5): 443. doi:10.1371/journal.pone.0000443 (www.plosone.org/doi/pone.0000443).

The following website has a helpful summary of the fruit fly study: Public Library of Science (2007, May 16). "Do Fruit Flies Have Free Will?" *ScienceDaily*. Retrieved May 25, 2012, from www.sciencedaily.com-/releases/2007/05/070516071806.html.

For more on the connections between animal behavior and free will, see B. Brembs, "Towards a Scientific Concept of Free Will as a Biological Trait: Spontaneous Actions and Decision-Making in Invertebrates", *Proceedings of the Royal Society B: Biological Sciences* 278 (2011): 930–39.

Libet discusses his work in the following article: Benjamin Libet, "Do We Have Free Will?", in Robert Kane (ed.), *Oxford Handbook of Free Will*, 1st edition (New York: Oxford University Press, 2002), 551–64.

For Daniel Wegner's claim that conscious will is an illusion, see Daniel Wegner, *The Illusion of Conscious Will* (Cambridge, MA: MIT Press, 2002).

For philosophical responses to Libet and Wegner, see Alfred Mele, *Effective Intentions: The Power of Conscious Will* (Oxford: Oxford University Press, 2009); Alfred Mele, "Free Will and Science", in Robert Kane (ed.), *Oxford Handbook of Free Will*, 2nd edition (New York: Oxford University Press, 2011), 499–514; and Eddy Nahmias, "Is Neuroscience the Death of Free Will?", *New York Times*, The Opinion Pages, www.opinionator.blogs. nytimes.com/2011/11/13/is-neuroscience-the-death-of-free-will.

8

WHERE DOES THIS LEAVE US?
SOME CONCLUDING THOUGHTS

THE ROLE OF PHILOSOPHY

In the last chapter, we looked at some scientific issues that relate to free will. We saw that science, though relevant, cannot tell us for sure whether we have free will or, if we do, what it is like. What about philosophy? Where do we end up after considering all of these philosophical positions, arguments, and objections? Do we have free will or don't we? Is free will possible? If so, how? Which theory makes the most sense? Why?

In this book, we have looked at all sorts of different views and their respective arguments: different versions of **compatibilism**, **libertarianism**, views that deny the existence of free will, and some others. Every view has its merits and its problems. You will notice that I have not taken a stand on which view is right or which arguments are successful. It is up to you to think about it and decide for yourself. But keep in mind that these are big questions – ones that you may revisit time after time and that you may change your mind about as you think through them. As with any other big philosophical problem, there are always more angles to ponder, more objections to respond to, and more questions to answer. A philosopher's work is never done!

Socrates (469–399 BCE), the great Ancient Greek philosopher and father of the Western philosophical tradition, emphasized the role of perplexity in gaining wisdom. He thought it was important to bring people to a state of confusion about big questions, such as "what is virtue?". So if you are still confused about free will, this is as it should be. Perplexity is important because it inspires you to keep thinking and to keep an open mind. Notice that you don't do much thinking about things that you feel confident that you know, and you don't think about things that seem perfectly clear to you.

Here's a famous philosophical example (not directly related to free will). You probably never think about whether there is a physical world outside of you. The existence of the physical world seems pretty clear to you and you feel confident that you know that the world exists. But if someone presents you with an argument as to why you can't be so sure about its existence, then you might become perplexed and start to think about it. René Descartes (1596–1650 CE) famously wonders how we can be sure at any given time that we aren't dreaming. Maybe all the things you see around you right at this moment are not "real" but just part of your dream. Maybe you are dreaming right now that you are reading this sentence. How can you be sure that you are not? There's no way to test it because any test you perform could just be part of your dream. Descartes also wonders how we can be sure that some evil genius is not manipulating us into thinking the world is real when really it is not. How could we know?

Very few people, philosophers included, really worry that the world does not exist or that everything is a dream. Even Descartes does not actually end up thinking that he's dreaming or that there's an evil genius manipulating him. But his arguments are supposed to make us wonder. They make us perplexed as to how or why we are so sure of these things. Descartes wants us to not take anything for granted when it comes to what we claim to know. And this perplexity opens our minds to new ways of thinking. In this case, it opens our minds to new ways of thinking about knowledge and how we come to know things. This is just one of many illustrations of the role of perplexity in philosophy. As I often remind my students, with philosophy, if you are not somewhat perplexed, you are probably not doing it right! It's like physical training for fitness or sports. You need to feel some exertion in order to make progress. When doing philosophy, you need to break a mental sweat!

But that doesn't mean you should be completely muddled. To continue the analogy, it's not "no pain, no gain". The aim is not injury. Philosophy is also about trying to gain clarity. I like to think that the idea is to try to get clearer on concepts, theories, and arguments – what are they? – while maintaining a sense of perplexity about their significance, their success, or their relationship to what we care about. In other words, you should be trying to gain clarity about what the different views of free will are, why these positions have been adopted, and how the arguments go. But you should also always be scratching your head and wondering "why"? Why is the problem of free will so hard to solve? Why does that solution seem right to me? Why might it be incorrect? Why do we think it's so important to have free will? Why is that argument really relevant to what we want to know? And so on.

Sometimes students become frustrated with philosophy because it seems not to provide any final answers. And you will notice that this book is the same way. It does not tell you whether we have free will, what free will *really* is, or which view is correct. A notable philosopher, Richard Taylor (1919–2003), provides some insight by drawing a distinction between knowledge and wisdom. Although it is controversial among philosophers just what knowledge is, how we come to know things, and how we know whether we know, one way of thinking of knowledge might be helpful to us in understanding Taylor's distinction. Some claims are verifiable in a way that gives them certainty, or at least something close to certainty. For example, take the following statements. *Human beings need oxygen in order to survive. Water = H_2O. George Washington was the first president of the United States.* These claims arguably count as things we know. They have been verified and are largely uncontroversial.

Though philosophers do not all agree about this, on one way of looking at it, much of philosophy is not about providing knowledge. Philosophy is about theories, concepts, and arguments. And as Taylor points out, we will never be certain if a philosophical theory is true or an argument sound in the way that we are certain about water or George Washington. (It's not that we cannot be wrong about these latter things, but the idea is that the latter have a different status than philosophical claims such as whether free will exists.) Philosophers have theories about the human mind or soul, theories about knowledge, and so on. There are arguments for God's existence, arguments against God's existence, arguments in favor of one ethical theory over another, and, of course, arguments for which theory of free will is the correct one. It only takes a smidgen of humility to realize that we will probably never have certainty about whether these kinds of arguments are successful.

But this is not to downplay the value of philosophy. Quite the contrary. Sometimes people will say that something is "just a theory" as if to downgrade its importance. This is not what is suggested here. Nor is the idea that there is no truth to be found. To claim that philosophy may not provide knowledge is not to say that it is not geared towards *truth*. Most philosophers working on the problem of free will and on many other philosophical problems believe that there is an objective truth. Many philosophers view their projects as part of a larger search for truth. The arguments and theories offered by philosophers are attempts to clarify, determine, or defend what seems true.

Sometimes students of philosophy will suppose that because they will not be told by their professor, for example, which theory is correct or what to believe, that therefore "anything goes". But this is a big mistake. There may be a plethora of positions and arguments concerning any given philosophical issue, but these positions and arguments are not all correct or sound. If you and I have mutually exclusive views, at least one of us is incorrect. It is really a misconception to think that "anything goes" in philosophy. Really, it's quite the opposite. An argument or theory has to be rigorously defended.

But although there is a truth to be found, the difficulty with philosophy is that our limited human perspective means that we cannot be absolutely sure when we've found it. We have to weigh the arguments, think it through, make provisional decisions about what we think, and keep looking into it. We can defend our positions, but we must keep our minds open to new objections and new ways of looking at an issue. In doing so, we gain wisdom. We gain a deeper understanding of the issues and arguments. We realize what we do not know. Socrates famously claimed that his wisdom consisted in knowing that he knew nothing. As we saw with perplexity, knowing what you do not know is also important in opening our minds to new ways of understanding. People who think they know everything are usually very reluctant to change their minds. Above all, we gain much from careful thinking. Perhaps we even gain insight into our own values.

As mentioned earlier, some philosophers will dispute Taylor's claim that philosophy does not aim to provide knowledge. There are some good arguments here as well. It is perhaps a bit ironic that philosophers do not even agree upon the aims of their own discipline! But the upshot here is largely the same. Even if philosophy is about providing knowledge, most philosophers will agree that it would be sheer hubris to suppose that we have reached certain knowledge on any of the big philosophical questions. But on this view, the process is still of great value because it enables us to get closer and closer to knowledge and it provides tremendous insight along the way. Consider the following analogy to theoretical physics. Presumably, theoretical physics does not provide us with certain knowledge concerning the origins of the universe, just as philosophy does not provide us with certain knowledge of free will. But the theoretical physicist does aim at knowledge with his theories, and his theorizing and search for the truth is of great value. Likewise with the philosopher. In both cases, the search for truth is important. At the *very least*, the search helps us figure out what we do not know. And that is no small feat.

All of this is to say that you should not look upon this book as the end of the story, but rather as the beginning. It is the beginning of a venture into pondering one of life's greatest questions.

CHOICES

I began this book with the idea that life is choices. Perhaps after reading this book you are beginning to wonder if this is actually true. Do we really have choices? After all, it seems that all the theories of free will have various difficult problems. And if we cannot find a theory to support free will, then it seems that we do not have *real* choices. I'd like to discuss the issue of choice one last time.

MUST WE CHOOSE?

Have you ever been faced with a very difficult life choice? How did you make your decision? Did you make it on your own? Did you ask someone else to make it for you? Famous existentialist philosopher Jean-Paul Sartre tells the story of a student who is faced with a difficult life decision. The student must decide whether to go to England and join the Free French Forces (to avenge his brother's death) or whether to stay home and help his mother, who would be lost without him. Sartre claims that he must choose, and he must choose on his own. One of Sartre's points here is that, in the end, no one can choose for us. If the student consults his professor with the idea of taking his professor's advice, this is a choice the student is making. The student has a good idea about what the professor will advise, so he has chosen to ask the professor, rather than asking someone else. Even if we suppose that the student does not know what the professor will say, the student must still choose whether to follow the advice. And he has still chosen to seek the advice. We cannot get out of such choices. Even if we flip a coin, or tell someone else to choose for us, we have chosen. We always, then, have the burden of choosing. We are, to use Sartre's phrase, "condemned to be free".

But can this be right if we do not have free will, as some theorists claim? I will not get into how to interpret Sartre's version of freedom or how to understand his intricate views of consciousness. But I think it is worth pointing out that Sartre is focused on a kind of subjective viewpoint here. Each of us is a subject. We have a certain perspective on the world because we are conscious and aware. And from the subjective stance, we must do something that at least looks an awful lot like choosing. Even the hard incompatibilist (the theorist who claims that we cannot have free will because it is incompatible with both **determinism** and **indeterminism**) can agree with this. After all, even the hard incompatibilist thinks about what to eat for breakfast, weighs the pros and cons of, say, corn flakes versus shredded wheat, and grabs the winning box of cereal. Some hard incompatibilists (such as Pereboom, whose view we discussed in Chapter 5) argue that we can deliberate even if we believe that determinism is true. We can still think through our options and try to figure out what is best.

And as Sartre emphasizes, these choices fall entirely on us, at least in a certain sense. Even if everything is predetermined and even if this rules out free will (a controversial claim, obviously), from a certain point of view, I must choose on my own. The idea is that from my perspective, there is a choice to be made. Regardless of whether determinism is true, or whether indeterminism is true and whether either of these rules out freedom, from my own standpoint, I must choose. When I am, say, filling out a questionnaire or taking an exam, I must decide how to fill in the blanks. It could be that determinism is true and how I fill in the blanks has been pre-ordained by a chain of causes. Or it could be that indeterminism is true and there is a measure of randomness in how I "choose" to fill them in. But nonetheless, from my point of view, I must choose. I cannot just let the world go on without me. Being passive is, in itself, a choice.

Some philosophers make a lot out of this idea of different standpoints, or different points of view. There is an objective, third-person point of view, and a subjective first-person point of view. So one way of understanding the current point is that at least from the subjective first-person point of view, we must make choices. If we look at ourselves "objectively", from a third-person stance, perhaps our choices are harder to countenance because they are, for example, either randomly occurring events, or the inevitable results of a causal chain, or what have you.

These are complicated issues. And it remains to be seen whether the idea of different points of view can be used to solve the problem of free will. But my point here is not to weigh in on whether this provides a solution, but instead to suggest a more practical message. That is, even if this book has convinced you that free will is impossible, you cannot get around the process of making "choices", whether or not these choices are genuine. From the practical point of view, then, it behooves each one of us to try to make the best choices we can, rather than thinking that it doesn't matter what choices we make, since there is no such thing!

WHY STUDY THE PROBLEM OF FREE WILL?

This practical message might make you wonder why it is so important to study the philosophical problem of free will. We looked at this question at the beginning of this book, but now it is worth revisiting. If, from my own personal standpoint, I must continue on and choose, then why worry about it at all? Why not forget all these philosophical musings, since at the end of the day, I must just go about my business? There are a number of ways of answering this question. One important concern is, again, **moral responsibility**. Some of the philosophers that we've studied will suggest that we want to know whether this first-personal "feeling" of choosing is indicative of genuine choice. We need the genuine variety in order to have real moral responsibility. And many people − not just philosophers − care about truth. We don't just want to feel as if we are choosing in a genuine sense. We want this to be true. So we want to see whether we can adequately justify a free will theory that supports this. In other words, it's not enough to have a choice-like experience. We want the choice to be *real*. Studying the problem of free will can give us insight into these kinds of issues. We can gain an understanding of what we think needs to be true in order for us to have such genuine choices. Does determinism need to be false? Or perhaps our choices need to be determined (in the right way)? Do we need **reasons-responsiveness**, the proper mesh among our internal states and our actions, inde-terministic dual efforts of will? In studying the problem of free will, we gain insight into what it means for something to be a real choice and under what conditions our choices are those for which we can be held morally responsible.

THE VALUE OF ACTING FREELY

In studying the problem of free will, we may also learn a great deal about what is important to us. What is it that we really care about when it comes to free will? Obviously, one thing we care about is moral responsibility. But what kind of free will do we value when it comes to moral responsibility? John Fischer puts it this way. He suggests that some people believe that what we care about is "making a difference". In other words, some of us suppose that the real value of acting freely is the value of having genuine alternatives and being able to choose between them. We may value being able to select the way the world will go from more than one option (this is what he and Ravizza call **regulative control**, discussed in Chapter 4). But others, such as Fischer, think that what we really value is not making a difference, but "making a statement" (this lines up with his account of **guidance control**, also discussed in Chapter 4). In other words, Fischer suggests that what we really want is to be able to engage in a kind of self-expression (he draws an analogy here to artistic expression, though he notes that the two are not exactly the same). On his view, we do not need to have genuine alternatives in order to express ourselves. We want to be able to make a statement, and doing so does not require alternatives. As Fischer puts it, in making a statement, I am writing a sentence in the book of my life. I am telling my story. According to Fischer, I do not need to be able to choose from multiple paths in order to do this.

These are not the only ways of thinking about what we might value about free will. But they should at least give you a lot to think about. Which do you care most about? Which do you think is the value of acting freely and the underlying value of moral responsibility? When it comes to the kind of free will required for moral responsibility, do you want to be free because you want to be able to express yourself, or do you want to be free because you want to "make a difference", in Fischer's sense? Or do you think that the value of acting freely is neither of these things? Or perhaps you think that self-expression *does* require alternatives, contrary to Fischer's claim.

There is a lot to be discussed here and much more to be said. But my point is that thinking about the problem of free will is not a stale theoretical exercise. It touches on our deepest concerns about who we are and who we want to be. Even if, from a practical standpoint, we must choose, reflecting on whether our choices are genuine and what needs to be true in order for them to be so, tells us a great deal about ourselves, our values, and our relations to one another.

FURTHER READING

For some useful background on Socrates, see Debra Nails, "Socrates", in Edward N. Zalta (ed.), *The Stanford Encyclopedia of Philosophy* (Spring 2010 Edition), www.plato.stanford.edu/archives/spr2010/entries/socrates. For an excellent book about Socrates' emphasis on perplexity and how perplexity relates to philosophy more generally, see Gareth Matthews, *Socratic Perplexity and the Nature of Philosophy* (New York: Oxford University Press, 2004).

For some useful background on Sartre, see Thomas Flynn, "Jean-Paul Sartre", in Edward N. Zalta (ed.), *The Stanford Encyclopedia of Philosophy* (Spring 2012 Edition), www.plato.stanford.edu/archives/

spr2012/entries/sartre/. For Sartre's example of the student and for some of Satre's most influential claims about freedom, see his famous essay: Jean-Paul Sartre, *Existentialism is a Humanism*, trans. Carol Macomber (New Haven, CT: Yale University Press [1946], 2007).

For some helpful background on Descartes, see Gary Hatfield, "René Descartes", in Edward N. Zalta (ed.), *The Stanford Encyclopedia of Philosophy* (Summer 2011 Edition), www.plato.stanford.edu/archives/sum2011/entries/descartes/. For Descartes' famous dreaming and evil genius arguments, see René Descartes, *Meditations on First Philosophy*, 3rd edition, trans. Donald A. Cress (Indianapolis, IN: Hackett, 1993).

An important and influential book that highlights the distinction between an objective and subjective stance and discusses its connection to different philosophical problems, including free will and agency, is: Thomas Nagel, *The View From Nowhere* (New York: Oxford University Press, 1989). For a view of action and action explanation that emphasizes a personal point of view versus an impersonal point of view, see Jennifer Hornsby, "Agency and Causal Explanation", in John Heil and Alfred Mele (eds), *Mental Causation* (New York: Oxford University Press, 1993), 161–88. For a compatibilist view of free will that emphasizes the distinction between a practical and a theoretical standpoint, see Hilary Bok, "Freedom and Practical Reason", in Gary Watson (ed.), *Free Will*, 2nd edition (New York: Oxford University Press, 2003), 130–66.

For more on John Fischer's discussion of the value of acting freely, see John Fischer, *My Way: Essays on Moral Responsibility* (New York: Oxford University Press, 2006); and John Fischer, *Our Stories: Essays on Life, Death, and Free Will* (New York: Oxford University Press, 2011).

GLOSSARY

agent causation (or agent-causal libertarianism): a theory of free will (usually a kind of **libertarianism**), according to which actions are caused directly by the agent as a **substance**, rather than by events occurring in the agent.

basic mental action: an action is basic if it is not a complex entity or process composed of other actions. A mental action is distinguished from an "overt" or bodily action. Depending on the theory, some examples of basic mental actions are choices, decisions, volitions (i.e. willings), and tryings. Sometimes a basic mental action stands alone. Other times it is the beginning of a more complex action. **Simple indeterminism** utilizes the notion of basic mental action.

causal powers: roughly, a causal power is the capacity to bring something about. Generally, an entity has causal powers in virtue of certain properties or attributes. Some versions of **agent-causal libertarianism** appeal to causal powers to argue that substances (i.e. persons) rather than events cause actions.

chaos theory: a scientific theory according to which small changes in a system lead to much larger effects. Popularly known as "the butterfly effect".

classical (or traditional) compatibilism: a kind of **compatibilism** espoused in the seventeenth and eighteenth centuries and again in the twentieth century. According to classical compatibilism, free will consists in the unhindered ability to do what one wants. The theory is often, though not always, paired with the **Conditional Analysis**.

compatibility: two things are compatible if they are possible together. Two statements are compatible if they can both be true together.

compatibilism: in free will, the theory that **determinism** does not rule out the kind of free will required for **moral responsibility.** Compatibilism is a view about the relationship between determinism and free will and does not necessarily involve a belief in determinism. See **soft determinism**.

Conditional Analysis: an analysis of "could have done otherwise" according to which "could have done otherwise" means "would have done otherwise if I had chosen to (or tried to, or wanted to)". This analysis of "could have done otherwise" is consistent with **determinism**, thus this analysis accompanies certain varieties of **compatibilism**.

Consequence argument: an argument for **incompatibilism**. If **determinism** is true, all of our actions follow inevitably from the past and the laws of nature. But no one is responsible or can do anything about the past and the laws of nature. Therefore no one can do anything about his actions (and therefore cannot be **morally responsible** for them).

counterexample: an example, usually fictitious, that is used to show that a general rule does not hold.

desert: deservingness. Moral desert centers on whether someone deserves praise or blame.

determinism (causal or nomological): a theory about the universe according to which the past and the laws of nature necessitate exactly the way the future will go in every detail. Some think of this theory in terms of cause and effect (hence, causal determinism).

Others use "nomological" to refer more generally to the **laws of nature** instead of focusing on cause and effect.

divine foreknowledge: God's infallible knowledge of everything that will happen, including what His creatures will do.

event-causal libertarianism: this version of **libertarianism** suggests that free actions are caused indeterministically by appropriate mental events within agents. When agents act freely, their actions are caused but not necessitated by their reasons, desires, or other appropriate entities. Robert Kane espouses one of the most important event-causal theories.

exceptionless regularities: according to some views of the **laws of nature**, the laws are exceptionless regularities. This means that things in the natural world happen in the same way, without exception.

first-order desires: desires for some other kind of object, such as a thing, state, or action; for example, a desire for cupcakes, a desire to be asleep, or a desire to go skiing (contrasted with **second-order desires**).

Frankfurt-style counterexamples: these are counterexamples to the **Principle of Alternative Possibilities (PAP)**. In these examples, the person does something that he wants to do and does it on his own, but there is another person standing by ready to intervene and force him to perform the action if it looks as if he is not about to do it. In these cases, we intuitively think the person is **morally responsible** even though he could not have done otherwise.

guidance control: this kind of control is distinguished from **regulative control**. It involves the ability to guide one's action but does not require that one can do otherwise. It emphasizes the "actual sequence" of action rather than the existence of alternative sequences. John Fischer and Mark Ravizza claim that guidance control is all that is needed for **moral responsibility** and they analyze guidance control in terms of moderate **reasons-responsiveness**.

hard determinism: a kind of **incompatibilism** according to which **determinism** is true and we never have free will.

hard incompatibilism: the view according to which we cannot have free will because free will is incompatible with both **determinism** and **indeterminism**.

illusionism: free will illusionism is the view, espoused by Saul Smilansky, that we have illusory beliefs about free will and that this is, for the most part, a good thing. We think we have libertarian free will (see **libertarianism**) but in fact we do not. But it is important for us to believe that we do in order to maintain belief in **moral responsibility** and to motivate us to do the right thing. Smilansky's view also involves a complex integration of **compatibilism** and **hard determinism**.

incompatibilism: in the free will context incompatibilism usually refers to the view that **determinism** rules out the kind of freedom required for **moral responsibility** (see **hard incompatibilism** for a variation).

incompatibility: two things are incompatible if they are not possible together or if they cannot both be true together.

indeterminism: a theory about the way the universe works according to which not everything is determined (though some things might be). Sometimes indeterminism may be used to refer to a particular process that does not involve necessitation, rather than referring to a theory about the universe.

laws of nature: the ways in which the natural universe operates. According to some theories, laws of nature are just descriptions of the way things have always happened. Other theories suggest that laws actually make things happen. Some philosophers see laws of nature as **exceptionless regularities**.

libertarianism: in the free will context, this is a kind of **incompatibilism** according to which **determinism** is false and we sometimes have free will (there are **event-causal**, **agent-causal**, and **simple indeterminist** varieties).

liberty of indifference: this refers to cases of free choice in which the agent is indifferent about his top alternatives. For example, if I want to buy some cereal, I may be indifferent about which of two perfectly good boxes of corn flakes I put in my cart.

logical determinism: the theory that the future is fixed because every proposition about the future already has a fixed truth value. If I say, "it will rain tomorrow", this is supposedly already true or false. Assume it is already true. Therefore, it must rain tomorrow.

logical fatalism: see **logical determinism**.

mechanism: this is the term used by John Fischer and Mark Ravizza to denote the process that leads to action or the way an action is caused. For example, in many cases, an action is caused by a "practical reasoning" mechanism. But acting from a compulsive desire would involve a different kind of mechanism.

mesh theories: mesh theories are a variety of **compatibilism**. These theories claim that freedom consists in an appropriate mesh between an action and the agent's inner states. One kind of mesh theory is the hierarchical theory of Harry Frankfurt, according to which freedom and responsibility are based on having the will one wants to have.

moral agency: in general, moral agency applies only to those beings who satisfy certain conditions, presumably certain intellectual and cognitive capacities that enable them to understand and engage in moral behavior (for example, the ability to understand the consequences of one's actions, the ability to see others as agents, the ability to evaluate one's own motives). Presumably, small children and animals do not possess moral agency, even though they possess agency of some sort.

moral agent: a being who is capable of undertaking and understanding moral behavior. See also **moral agency**.

moral responsibility: there are different accounts of moral responsibility. In general, to say that someone is morally responsible means that he can be praised or blamed for his behavior. On a deeper account, this means that he *deserves* praise or blame. On a shallower notion, this means that praise and blame are appropriate because they are useful for shaping future behavior. Some theories of responsibility utilize the notion of **reactive attitudes**. Someone who is morally responsible must be an appropriate target of these attitudes.

mysterianism: free will mysterianism is the view that we cannot give up our belief in free will, but we also are unable to figure out how free will is possible, since it appears to be contradictory. It appears to be incompatible with both **determinism** and **indeterminism**.

phenomenal quality: the way something seems or feels to us, that is, how we experience it. Carl Ginet's version of **simple indeterminism** utilizes the notion of an "actish phenomenal quality". He claims that our uncaused **basic mental actions** feel like actions, that is, they feel as if we are making them happen.

Principle of Alternative (or Alternate) Possibilities (PAP): according to this principle, a person acted freely (or morally responsibly) only if he could have done otherwise.

Principle of Universal Causation: the theory that every event must have a cause (nothing is uncaused).

probabilistic causation: the theory that at least some causes do not necessitate their effects but merely make them more likely. Sometimes also called indeterministic causation.

problem of luck, the: some philosophers worry that if an action is not determined, then it seems like a matter of chance or luck that it occurred rather than an alternative action that could have occurred instead. This is a potential problem for **libertarianism**.

psychological determinism: roughly, this is the view that our behavior is determined by our psychology. Psychological determinism can be distinguished from causal or nomological determinism (see **determinism [causal or nomological]**). Psychological determinism could be true, but causal determinism false (for example, there could be some indeterministic processes in the world, such as radioactive decay, but our behavior could still be fully determined by our psychology).

reactive attitudes: P.F. Strawson's theory that interpersonal relations involve certain natural human attitudes such as indignation, anger, gratitude, affection, and so on. According to Strawson and others, whether someone can be appropriately held morally responsible depends upon whether he is the appropriate target of such attitudes.

real self (or deep self) views: these views are a kind of **compatibilism**. They base freedom and responsibility on whether the will or the action comes from something the agent identifies with as part of his real desires. On such views, an agent acts with free will when what he does expresses his "real self". Harry Frankfurt's hierarchical mesh theory is an example of a real self view (see **mesh theories**).

reason explanations: explanation for action in terms of an agent's reasons for performing it. Philosophers debate over whether these explanations must be causal. Some say that one's reasons must be causes. Others suggest that reasons are not causes but can still explain the action (perhaps such explanations are **teleological explanations**).

reasons–responsiveness: being appropriately sensitive to the reasons presented by the world. Putting it roughly, reasons-responsiveness means that had other reasons (favoring a different action) presented themselves, then the action would have differed accordingly. On the other hand, if I have a compulsion or neurotic disorder such that I would do what I am doing no matter what other reasons presented themselves, then I am not reasons-responsive. Reasons-responsiveness is connected to **guidance control**, a kind of **compatibilism** espoused by John Fischer and Mark Ravizza.

Reason View: Susan Wolf's version of **compatibilism**. According to her view, it is not enough for an agent to be acting from his real self (see **real self views**). The agent must be able to see the world the way it really is. He must be able to recognize what is actually good and be able to do the right thing for the right reasons.

regulative control: this kind of control involves alternative possibilities – i.e. being able to do otherwise. **Traditional incompatibilism** and some kinds of **compatibilism** (compatibilism that utilizes the **Conditional Analysis**) involve a belief that regulative control is required for responsibility.

revisionism: revisionism about free will is the view that our concept of free will is not accurate and must be revised in order to accord with our current understanding of the phenomenon. On Manuel Vargas' particular version of revisionism, our current concept is libertarian (see **libertarianism**) of a kind that requires genuine alternatives, but needs to be revised because such a concept is not plausible given what we now know.

second-order desires: desires that have other desires as objects; for example, wanting to want to exercise, wanting to not want to smoke. Distinguished from **first-order desires**.

second-order volitions: Harry Frankfurt's term for desires about one's will. One's will is a desire that moves one all the way to action. See also **first-order desires** and **second-order desires**.

self-forming actions (SFAs): This is Robert Kane's term for those actions that help us form our own characters. According to Kane, a proponent of **event-causal libertarianism**, when we are faced with certain important decisions, it is undetermined which choice we will make. We may be torn between two options. By deciding, we help to shape our character and influence future choices.

semi-compatibilism: This term is coined by John Fischer to refer to the view whereby **determinism** is (or is most likely) incompatible with the ability to do otherwise, but is compatible with the kind of freedom required for **moral responsibility**. Such a view therefore does not seek to provide a compatibilist analysis of "could have done otherwise". See **Conditional Analysis**.

simple indeterminism: a kind of **libertarianism** that claims that all free actions either are, or begin with, uncaused **basic mental actions**.

soft determinism: a kind of **compatibilism** that holds that **determinism** is true and that we sometimes have free will.

source incompatabilism: in general, this kind of **incompatibilism** holds that **determinism** threatens free will because it rules out the ability of an agent to be the ultimate source of her actions. The existence of alternatives is not the issue. The **Principle of Alternative Possibilities** could be false and **Frankfurt-style counterexamples** to it could be successful. But determinism is still a threat.

substance: an individual object or entity, usually distinguished from events and from properties (i.e. qualities or attributes). Depending on the theory, examples of substances are ordinary objects like pencils and chairs, animals, persons, and stuffs (like water or acid). **Agent causation** claims that actions involve substance causation. In other words, actions are caused by persons as substances.

teleological explanations: teleological explanations are explanations in terms of the goal or purpose of something. For example, if someone wants to know why my computer has speakers, a teleological explanation will cite the purpose of the speakers. It has speakers so that users can listen to sounds coming from their computers. Some philosophers suggest that reasons for acting provide teleological explanations. See **reason explanations**.

theological determinism (or theological fatalism): the theory that God has perfect foreknowledge, therefore everything that God foreknows (including what we will do) must occur.

traditional incompatabilism: according to traditional **incompatibilism**, the **Principle of Alternative Possibilities** is true. **Determinism** threatens free will/responsibility because it rules out alternatives. This is distinguished from **source incompatibilism**.

INDEX

American Philosophy in *The Basics*

American Philosophy: The Basics

Nancy Stanlick, University of Central Florida, USA

American Philosophy: The Basics introduces the history of American thought from early Calvinists to the New England Transcendentalists and from contract theory to contemporary African American philosophy. The key question it asks is: what it is that makes American Philosophy unique? This lively and compelling book moves through key periods in the development of American thought from the founding fathers to the transcendentalists and pragmatists to contemporary social commentators. Readers are introduced to:

- Some of the most important thinkers in American history including Jonathan Edwards, Thomas Paine, Charles Sanders Pierce, Thomas Kuhn, Cornel West and many more
- Developments in five key areas of thought: epistemology, metaphysics, religion and ethics, social philosophy, and political philosophy
- The contributions of American women, African-Americans and Native Americans.

Featuring suggestions for further reading and assuming no prior knowledge of philosophy, this is an ideal first introduction for anyone studying or interested in the history of American thought.

November 2012 – 180 pages
Pb: 978-0-415-68970-0 | Hb: 978-0-415-68972-4

For more information and to order a copy visit
www.routledge.com/9780415689700

Available from all good bookshops

Artificial Intelligence: The Basics

Kevin Warwick, University of Reading, UK

"This book is authoritatively and enthusiastically written by one of the leading experts in the field. It is academically rigorous but eminently readable ... This is a great book for those looking for a concise, up-to-date introduction to AI." – *Dr. Patrick Hill, BCS - The Chartered Institute for IT, UK*

Artificial Intelligence: The Basics is a concise and cutting-edge introduction to the fast moving world of AI. The author Kevin Warwick, a pioneer in the field, examines issues of what it means to be man or machine and looks at advances in robotics which have blurred the boundaries. Topics covered include:

- how intelligence can be defined
- whether machines can 'think'
- sensory input in machine systems
- the nature of consciousness
- the controversial culturing of human neurons.

Exploring issues at the heart of the subject, this book is suitable for anyone interested in AI, and provides an illuminating and accessible introduction to this fascinating subject.

August 2011 – 184 pages
Pb: 978-0-415-56483-0 | Hb: 978-0-415-56482-3

Bioethics: The Basics

Alastair Campbell, National University of Singapore

Bioethics: The Basics is an introduction to the foundational principles, theories and issues in the study of medical and biological ethics. Readers are introduced to bioethics from the ground up before being invited to consider some of the most controversial but important questions facing us today. Topics addressed include:

- the range of moral theories underpinning bioethics
- arguments for the rights and wrongs of abortion, euthanasia and animal research
- healthcare ethics including the nature of the practitioner-patient relationship
- public policy ethics and the implications of global and public health.

Concise, readable and authoritative, this is the ideal primer for anyone interested in the study of bioethics.

July 2013 – 224 pages
Pb: 978-0-415-50408-9 | Hb: 978-0-415-50409-6

Philosophy: The Basics
5th Edition

Nigel Warburton

"*Philosophy: The Basics* deservedly remains the most recommended introduction to philosophy on the market. Warburton is patient, accurate and, above all, clear. There is no better short introduction to philosophy."
– Stephen Law, author of *The Philosophy Gym*

Philosophy: The Basics gently eases the reader into the world of philosophy. Each chapter considers a key area of philosophy, explaining and exploring the basic ideas and themes including:

- Can you prove God exists?
- How do we know right from wrong?
- What are the limits of free speech?
- Do you know how science works?
- Is your mind different from your body?
- Can you define art?
- How should we treat non-human animals?

For the fifth edition of this best-selling book, Nigel Warburton has added an entirely new chapter on animals, revised others and brought the further reading sections up to date. If you've ever asked 'what is philosophy?', or wondered whether the world is really the way you think it is, this is the book for you.

November 2012 – 184 pages
Pb: 978-0-415-69316-5 - Hb: 978-0-415-69317-2

For more information and to order a copy visit:
http://www.routledge.com/9780415693165

Available from all good bookshops

www.routledge.com/books/series/B

Religion and Science in *The Basics*

Religion and Science: The Basics

Philip Clayton, Claremont School of Theology and Claremont Lincoln University, USA

Religion and science are arguably the two most powerful social forces in the world today. But where religion and science were once held to be compatible, most people now perceive them to be in conflict. This unique book provides the best available introduction to the burning debates in this controversial field. Examining the defining questions and controversies, renowned expert Philip Clayton presents the arguments from both sides, asking readers to decide for themselves where they stand:

- science or religion, or science and religion?
- Intelligent Design vs. New Atheism
- the role of scientific and religious ethics – designer drugs, AI and stem cell research
- the future of science vs. the future of religion.

Viewpoints from a range of world religions and different scientific perspectives are explored, making this book essential reading for all those wishing to come to their own understanding of some of the most important debates of our day.

August 2011 – 196 pages
Pb: 978-0-415-59856-9 – Hb: 978-0-415-59855-2